Black Male Feminism

Michael Marsden, PhD

2019

Black Male Feminism

First Printing: 2019

ISBN 978-1-7337455-2-9

i&R Publishing
7979 Broadway #209
San Antonio, TX 78209

https://iandrpublishing.wordpress.com

Ordering Information:
Special discounts are available on quantity purchases by corporations, associations, educators, and others. For details, contact the publisher at the above listed address.

To Kaiser and Vanessa H. for showing me new methods
in rebellion.

Contents

Black Male Feminism   ix

1. My First Encounters with Feminism

Eight years ago, while walking me through the preparation steps for my first year as a college cultural diversity instructor, a colleague of mine Brad landed on the topic of feminism. "Yeah, I identify as a feminist," he said. "A man can be a feminist too." He then told me a little bit more about his background in social scholarship, his wife, and the progressive stance that undergirded much of his work. Trained by my previous schooling never to dismiss another person's perspective, I had no doubt that Brad meant what he said, found his explanation to be reasonable, and left it at that as we moved onto other topics. That single brief comment in our discussion would ultimately have a major effect on me over the years, however, as I gradually came to research feminism myself for inclusion in my cultural diversity curriculum.

Over the next seven years I found my lectures on feminism to be among the most consistently enjoyable classes for me to teach and among the most eye-opening for my students. Who knew that feminism had three official "waves" (plus one unofficial one at the time)?

① First Encounters

Who knew that the feminism known by many
non-feminists—bra burning and all that—was really a
staple of second wave feminism's call for respect, while
the first wave was mainly about the right to vote?
Meanwhile, the third wave is all about increasingly
sophisticated academic research alongside a more
popularly recognized upsurge of "girl-power." And the
growing fourth wave revolves around gendered social and
political inclusiveness.

Time and again I began these lectures by asking my
students *What do you know about feminists?* They hate
men. They want equal rights. They protest. It's from here
that we'd set off each time on another four-hour journey
to clear up the mystery: Feminism is not just about
women screaming at men for a pie slice. Nor is it solely
about equal rights for the sexes. For those of us up on
LGBTQ issues, you know that feminism isn't even 100%
about women. Instead, feminism is more generally about
broader power dynamics and about how a failure to
acknowledge power inequities in one area costs a whole
society its long-term potential in other areas. You can
advance your economy and your technology all day, but if
your class structure is broken, the fear of losing power
will come back to bite you on the all kinds of
levels—educational, humanitarian, political,
environmental, and medical—as the haves must

increasingly carry the burden of the have-nots whose lives they own. In his landmark book *Wealth of Nations*, Adam Smith called slavery economically "inefficient," because the master must pay for a whole person rather than just paying a subsistence level wage.[1] The effects are similar for slavery in the social sense. When we speak of feminism, we speak of a call to end the oppression of those who are taught to connect first at the hands of those who are taught to force first—an end to a culture that diminishes long term cooperation in favor of short term bursts of power. At least that's how I would eventually come to see it as I gradually began to adopt my own non-macho views of how to respond to things.

Encountering less aggressive options

I'll never forget that day in class where I asked my students, "Who in here mainly uses dominance to resolve conflict?" About 2/3 of the class proudly raised their hands. "Okay, who in here uses passivity?" Only three out of 30 raised their hands, including a giant black guy sitting in the back corner. "Interesting," I replied. "I do too. And why do you use this method that most of us Americans are taught to see as weak?" His answer: *Because I don't wanna get sent up again* (to prison that is). And there you have it. In a society which celebrates extremes, retaliation, and the contagious spread of outrage, there are some of us who simply pay a higher price for showing such outrage. Especially as a college teacher who—in his younger years—was made to pay for a colorful array of others' tales that mostly never happened, I've had to learn a number of non-macho ways of handling obstacles. Listen first. Don't let aggression (or even a reaction) be your only option. Make the domain yours. Then write the rules within that domain. And although this sequence isn't necessarily feminine, it's not nearly as traditional-masculine as our Western education has taught us males to be.

About a decade ago I formally adopted Daoism as my life philosophy along with some of Buddhist thought. I've shifted greatly in the friends I keep, from a more activist group to a more opportunity-building one. All in all, the "passive" groups I keep today are MUCH stronger as people, as personalities, and as social influencers than I could have handled years prior, and the analogy I like to make is that of the strong guy, the corporate executive, and the common citizen: When I was young I learned that "only the strong survive," overpowering the weak. Later I learned that the executive could instantly wipe out the gains of thousands of "strong" people at once with a series of signatures. Now I know that the reactions of the right groups of "weak citizens" can drive entire economic systems full of corporations into the toilet, or elevate others to monopoly. How much it pays to throw my masculinity around will depend on where I am in that chain. A passive man today may control the careers of thousands tomorrow.

Being male isn't that bad, but...

Having said the above, I love being male, am proud of my many classic male ways, and am writing this book with the intent that other males should gain a valuable tool for surviving a world which too easily crushes that male pride. For any of us who have ever had that girlfriend who provoked you near the point of no return, for those who've done the assertive thing only to face a rumor mill or family gang-up far stronger than any dominant thing we could think of, for any who—no matter how much of a man they tried to be—simply could not get hired, couldn't carry all the bills, or couldn't serve his family without giving up his own self-respect, this book is for you.

The reason we males on the whole have been having a hard time thriving under the new maze of social punishments is not because we aren't tough enough, but because we are actively discouraged from using the full set of tools that women are increasingly encouraged to use. We pay for the crimes of the patriarchs before us, but lack the social currency to draw upon for bringing down that debt. 21st century Western women are allowed to be nurturing, spiritual, and (when called for) passive. But they are also allowed to be tough, body-proud, and in command. For 21st century men, nurturing is mainly limited to dads, spirituality is weird, and being passive is derided if you claim to be straight.

Imagine a world in which female-types are allowed to display both masculine and feminine characteristics while the male-types who still run many of our struggling social systems are denied public attention *unless* they've gotten it through a fight. Imagine how difficult it will be to achieve true sex equality if the males in a position to legislate via listening are mocked for doing so. That's where we are in the early 21st century. Masculinity has been cornered by a system of social pressures which uses both masculinity and femininity. As a group often given the least respect among mainstream ethnicities, blacks provide one of the clearest cases of such social confinement.

Black males have the interesting status of being expected—even encouraged—to behave loudly, provocatively within those confines. But a boxer doesn't spend the whole bout throwing punches. Sometimes he has to block. Provocation without observation will leave us face down. Demonstration without cooperation will keep all males—not just black males—in a cage. Caged males can only open so many political doors for the females who greet them. And society as a whole fails to mature past a certain point. Why am I a feminist? Because I've learned to recapture my full male pride by giving myself the option of occasionally turning my male tactics **off**. No corporation, no rumor mill, no man nor woman can pressure me into screwing myself. But in order to get here I've needed to face all that I bring to the table and be proud of it—including the push for equal air time for non-macho tactics among us men.

Where gendered power dynamics are concerned, I see our society as being crippled by an excess of two things: blind male machismo and pseudo-female assertion disguised as a certain kind of "third wave" girl-power. Masculinity isn't the problem, but insecure masculinity is. Girl-power isn't the problem, but commoditized girl-power isn't feminism. It's just another vehicle for masculine political systems and industries to exploit on a wider scale. Said another way, being masculine doesn't automatically mean your decisions make sense for you as a male; outfighting the male near you doesn't mean you've achieved equality as a female. Both of these cases define the male and female in terms of the male-centric standard of "bad-assedness." As for listening to others, learning more about what's going on before we tweet, clarifying the other's position before we launch the latest remix of our own, neither American boys nor American girls are taught enough of this. Unfortunately, there are only two groups of people who are equipped to make effective change to these kinds of assertion-(mis)writing systems: The first consists of the empowered subjects of power—particularly, feminists and their supporters operating under the patriarchy. The second group consists of males who are able and willing to write systemic change from within, regardless of their total agreement with those who seek it.

The need for better paths

The short answer to why males should support feminism beyond the basic bleeding-heart argument "for our mothers and daughters" is as follows: Because you as male don't like wrong-headed systems—which are not your own—blocking your opportunities in society.[2] Forget about our male training to think of feminists as being man-haters. If we want to replace the mutated-capitalist, politically contentious, policy-revolving hamster wheel with actual progress on the individual level, we as males will re-open the discussion of what it means to define our masculinity rather than having definitions put upon our homes and families from lofty institutions above. This is closer to second and fourth wave feminism. Why does feminism matter? Because the power dynamics of collective discussion, long-range planning, and gap-closing begin with a look beyond the traditional template for cutting hair with a chainsaw. Masculine ways work, but not without feminine counterbalance. Feminine ways work, but not by simultaneously hijacking and stepping on the very masculinity that circumscribes both. Feminism is important because having balanced options for power is important. For males and females alike who wish to create a future in which they, rather than their industrial and governmental masters, can control their own social fates, we have a foundation in the feminist cause which gets to the heart of self-determination. Men and women alike need other weapons besides the macho—just in case the macho threatens to blow up whatever we're building.

2. How a Male Becomes Feminist

This chapter outlines the kinds of experiences that can turn a temperamental, straight male into a temperamental, straight male feminist. "Own it" is what I say, and I hope this chapter prompts the males who read it to think about the kinds of things they truly identify with, independent of social pressure. There are plenty of things that can shape a man's persona which he's just not allowed to talk about, so I talk about them here to let you know: It's alright to deviate from the advertised "male ideal." Knowing ourselves is the first stage in accessing our full power as men.

One of my favorite ideas in Chinese philosophy is that "a thing at its maximum turns into its opposite." At the moment when every last packet of daylight has been issued forth, we have night. A ruler with limitless dominion replaces all of his citizens with mere extensions of his own puppetry. Thus he rules no one. A man in prison can feel his masculine urges so strongly that he makes other men into his power subjects—violating one of the common assumptions of normal-world masculinity. A thing at its maximum can, by the nature of what it means to be at maximum, expand no more without changing its own nature.

I remember first being struck in high school by this idea that hypermasculinity can actually lead to a reduction in masculinity. There, I met my first and last open homophobe. To make a long story short, this kid was so deliberately anti-gay that it made him seem weak in a way me and my friends couldn't put our finger on. We said something like "Dude, what's the big deal? Did a gay person turn you down or something?" I mean it's not like he had to prove anything to us. Nobody cared that much. But this guy. His extreme homophobia was really pretty weird, and certainly didn't make him any more male in our eyes.

For me, masculinity has always been a matter of pushing into the unknown. You are masculine to the extent that you don't revert to a process-response model in cases where you'd really rather act-receive, and you act-receive by default in new situations. So **masculinity** is defined here as, by default, **giving priority to acting first, receiving feedback second in the situations one approaches**. I define **femininity** as, by default, **giving priority to receiving information first, acting second in the situations one approaches**. Ideas or situations which have a "shoot first" character are what I call masculine-element ideas.

Curse words which cut through the regular level
of normatively pasteurized linguistic exchange,

MASCULINE square shapes whose corners assert their
ELEMENT importance as the limiter of line, and

governments which thrive on speeches, missiles,
and police powers

are all masculine-element for their ability to declare
themselves against their less stubborn negative space
(where the ability to arouse our attention is concerned).
The male penis is also masculine not just because it is a
central feature of standard male bodies, but because it
serves as a jagged protrusion in the otherwise flowing
male silhouette. Like a Dirac delta.

Meanwhile,

curved shapes,

education,

FEMININE
ELEMENT town halls, and

vaginas

are examples of feminine-element ideas because the
people who observe them typically follow the general
form (or flow) around these things *before* their character

can be properly described. **Masculine-elements are described by their assertive features**. Feminine-elements are described by the observations which their wholes elicit. Male is a biology predisposed towards masculine expression: action in the face of the unknown. Female is a biology predisposed towards feminine expression: creation of an action in light of a complementary interaction. Just because a biology says something, however, doesn't mean the mind or the sociological preferences have to agree with it. Thus we have the basis of sex-atypical characteristics of various kinds.

Preferences which aren't always macho

In my unending self-questioning I've adopted several identities which are the feminine versions of their "normal" American equivalents.

- First and foremost, I am a dedicated oldest brother to two exceptional gentleman as younger brothers *before* I am a macho man. So I'm a nurturer first, regardless of what rap told me.

- As I went through middle school I started asking what I believed about the world independent of what other folks who looked like me were saying. Today I am a Buddhist-Daoist and not a Christian, with an *internal* spirituality rather than a more person-to-person one.

- As a certain kind of Buddhist I am also a type atheist, not agnostic or a believer. So my governing authority is a receptive state of being rather than an acting personality. (There are at least 4 kinds of atheists: atheists, nihilists, non-theists, and abstract pantheists whose highest authority is more like an abstract potential-space under which the familiar world sits. The last one is more Hindu, and the one I identify with. This kind of thing mainly affects how and where you think your incentives to be a better person come from.)

- I fall in love at first sight for nearly every girl I interact with closely.

  - But having been flustered by my own weaknesses in this area I've learned to heavily distrust sex and refuse to dive into the chaos of dating.

  - Then again I'm a die-hard toucher. A toucher who doesn't really like people in his personal space. I treat having sex with someone as giving them all the keys to everything I own—*especially* my creativity.

  - And I'm stingy as hell with my creativity.

- I love spirituality and astrology, and get easily teary-eyed over old movies and romantic comedies.

  - On the other hand, most of the male-female mating dance, standard entertainment, and the typically advertised American social life make my blood boil when foisted upon me...Like being a black man with a basketball shoved into his hand from birth:

  - The endless stress and masculine ego of basketball isn't for me, but I love interesting social statistics.

- Lastly, I am a heterosexual man who knows full well that there are those corners where another male would probably be able to break into his space. One of those corners is in prison. The other is in certain very improbable—but still possible—D/s (Domination/submission) cases with a woman as the 2nd person and a non-masculine male as the 3rd person, assisting with the woman. Lie to yourself if you like about this kind of thing, but the prison example is tough to realistically plan for.

I forgot to mention that I'm polyamorous with a real respect for actual (as opposed to Hollywood) BDSM. But I have a deathly allergy towards most kinds of heteronormative monogamy. As you'll see shortly, this last area of sexual self-definition actually forms a core component of my feminism.

Ever since puberty, I've had this habit of reaching for a second female partner as soon as I've found the first one. I've never cheated, am too self-confident to lie (a.k.a. turning my back on a decision I've made), and yet I formerly described my second-girl habit as "serial emotional cheating" because these were the kinds of attachments which I knew would make Girl #1 jealous if she knew the extent of it. To get around the inconvenience of hiding stuff from my partners and myself, I've had only "friends with benefits," never an actual girlfriend, and always told everyone involved. As I've gotten older and more jaded with certain women's games however, I've learned to enjoy basic flirting even more than any kind of formal attachment. My early sexual experiences came very late and were very bad, as I earned the not-so-coveted "minuteman" status with my partner. This dealt a deep blow to my heteronormalized manhood, and ended in my throwing a partnership-killing temper tantrum in two of those relationships. Ironically though, my first and biggest man-failure of this kind was followed by a series of encounters which changed my life: I still remember Leah and Jess, Colin, Shannon, Fred and Oram—whose brief encounters pushed me away from the romantic and into the intellectual-platonic. They made it okay for me to define myself in terms of how I treated others rather than how I lived up to some template for how males like me ought to "be."

I lost my virginity at 23 (a near-geriatric age for black males as I understand it) and in the decade following I had a lot to learn about how much I was willing to give and how much I was willing to take regarding this aspect of a relationship. Over the course of the next couple of years and the next couple of partners, I learned that—as in all other areas of my life—I hated feeling disempowered. I hated hooking up with girls who wanted a fuck buddy but showed no interest in what I liked. I hated being obligated to take these kinds of girls out, hated spending money on them and—even worse—*time* on them, and hated pretending to enjoy myself when my real interest was in plain old quality bonding without the scripted social noise surrounding it. As a naturally high-strung person, I learned that reaching orgasm quickly (the "minuteman" problem) was only a problem with girls I didn't trust, but there was no such problem with girls whom I *did* trust. Totally psychological. I also learned that, as an amorous person, I had to watch out for a tendency to flirt with my students in the first few years of teaching college. Never did I break any rules or do anything that I couldn't defend against, but I know I allowed breaches in the *spirit* of the fraternization policy more times than I could count. Naturally amorous, I was that "kid in a candy store"—teaching plenty of sexy, smart and funny girls his age. And my female students flirted with me many more times than the other way around. My biggest crime was closer to not stopping it than anything else. All this changed, however, around the time I turned 34 and had to teach a psychology class.

Where the change began

Our school only offered PSYC201 once in rare while, and I was basically the only one who taught it. During one particular semester I had a whopping six students, all of whom enjoyed talking about relationships more than the usual bunch. As part of the preparation for the class, I found a book called *The Sexual Spectrum* by Dr. Olive Skene Johnson.[3] It was through this book that I became painfully aware of my thorough ignorance regarding most things non-hetero. Together our entire class (including myself) learned more about relationships, elementary kink, how it is not biologically or even psychologically possible to be 100% straight, and taboo areas of the male and female body. (Yes male bodies do contain estrogen, and female bodies do produce testosterone.) Other topics included the off-limits issue of penis size and the male preoccupation with it, male and female shaming, and even love languages. It was during this class that I learned that my "serial emotional cheating" was actually called polyamory, and from there I became an off-the-record sexologist with a concentration on power-dynamics. I hadn't arrived at feminism yet, but was approaching feminist territory from the male side.

How a male can end up cornered through no fault of his own

While I was learning more about polyamory, meeting other polys, and getting the feel for the culture, a long-standing relationship of mine was coming to a close. If open communication lies at the heart of a good relationship, my eight year association with my beloved Lila had eroded dramatically over the years. This culminated in one last tryst after which she retreated to her customary silence from her base in another city, and I—for the first time—was made to feel something I never imagined I could ever feel.

Though there are few things that bother me to talk about, my last sexual experience with Lila remains a dark chapter for me. Having been considered a weird person all my life, I've been accused of harassment, called out on creepy mannerisms, made sudden off-color remarks which have literally left me homeless for days, jobless, but mostly just avoided. I've been seen as a weirdo by behavior, and even dangerous in my younger displays of explosive temper, but never would I hurt anyone intentionally—not even for revenge. Like lying, intentionally doing something to hurt someone goes against my ego as a rational being and my pride as an oldest brother/caretaker. But the months following my last day with Lila were very difficult for me. She had always been withdrawn, distant as a person, and yet timelessly beautiful to me no matter what her other issues in life were. And she had many serious ones. Still, I had always been there for Lila in whatever way I could be, even after she left me in Texas for other adventures. I cared for her with everything I had, and truly did love her with all my heart.

One afternoon, Lila visited me in San Antonio. She had only a day, and I had to work in the middle of it. Early in the morning we talked about things, I watched her work on her art as she always did, and eventually we settled into each other's arms as we had so many times before. There was some conversation, but soon I had to leave for a three hour teaching shift. Three hours became four. Four became five. And I eventually returned home 5½ hours later to find her curled up on my couch, clearly in deep thought about something. For the next hour I held her, we talked, and she revealed some things about her past which she had never told me in the eight years I had known her. For one, our relationship had begun with me as the "other man." She had cheated on whoever this was and, I guess, at some point replaced him with me. She told me about her subsequent relationships in the time she had spent out of Texas, what she had been through, and told me how those experiences had made her feel dirty, taken advantage of, though also empowered in some way. She told me how she felt she didn't deserve me and how she had betrayed me so many times. In turn, I told her that none of this mattered to me. We had never been formally committed to begin with, but simply liked and supported each other. She had always been free to do whatever she wanted and see anyone else she wanted, but I wasn't really up for letting her drag past demons into our moment.

So we made love as "Capprichio Arabe" and Sarah Jarosz' "Mile on the Moon" played in the background; the afternoon had fully arrived as the sun shone through the glass sliding door behind us and this petite little girl—with all her dry surface wit and infinitely tangled inner world—proceeded to once again be more beautiful a soul to me than any goddess. At least it started that way.

Soon love turned to sex, which then turned to fucking. But this time was different. Although we had been together many times before, today she was on her period. And there was blood. I knew that at some point something had come over her, and when she pushed me away right in the middle of some of her most intense writhing, I pulled back because she didn't normally do this. I saw Lila's blood for the first time—a sight I had never seen before with any girl—and would later have to look up what it meant. But by this point she had gone from seemingly euphoric to very, very sad. There were tears in her eyes which lightly streaked down her face, but I don't think she cried. I looked at her, then looked down again. I looked her in her eyes again and told her "It's okay. It's okay." For me, nothing had changed. But she started to get up. I held her hand and asked her stay. She did, and we talked for a little while more. Soon after though, she got dressed and decided it was time for her to make the long drive back home. As we parted ways at my door I remember telling here. "I want you to be happy. Smile babe. I don't want you to leave here upset. You promise?" She smiled, we exchanged another soft kiss standing at my doorway, and that was it.

But the weeks that followed were some of the toughest I have ever experienced.

Although I'd had eight years to get used to Lila's long spells of non-communication, this time was different. Immediately after Lila left, I felt dirty. As if I had raped her. I became angry that our lovemaking, which had begun in the same passionate way as it had many times before, had all of a sudden given rise to a sadness which I wasn't *allowed* to understand. Somewhere in the middle of our time together, Lila had transformed from my dearest love to some stranger imposed upon by a dick. One minute we were in passionate embrace and literally the next minute she was unreachable. I worried that she didn't love me anymore. I worried that her family would drive a wedge between us—"That savage black guy you fuck isn't good enough for our saintly Hispanic sister." I was frustrated when, upon calling her, I got no answer. But instead got a text saying "My sister's here and I'm not talking to anyone right now." I thought to myself, *Goddammit Lila, you don't just make a guy who loves you so much feel like he's violated you and not say anything to ease his mind.* I thought this last case of non-communication was so much more unfair to me than she'd ever been. Cheating I can handle. Her other issues I could handle. But making me complicit in her suffering via the closest moment we knew how to share was unfair. I thought of how people who knew nothing about me and Lila might respond to ANY account of that afternoon. How a city full of semi-random sub-surface prejudice like San Antonio could truly <u>invent</u> an entire story about "what black male Michael did to Lila." Stories like that have happened before and, of course, ruined the lives of the falsely accused. And the thought made me angry.

Even though nothing even remotely close to abuse had occurred then or ever, I realized that I couldn't tell anyone about how I felt because the mere use of the word "rape" to describe how her behavior made *me* feel would raise all sorts of red flags in whomever I told. All because she was unusually sad after sex and went quiet for weeks afterwards—with no attempt to talk to me about anything. The usual weeks of silence that I'd had years to get used to, ate me up this time.

I'd been the victim of a false sexual harassment complaint before. As a male there is almost nothing you can do but accept the punishment by an uncritical mass of people in their armchairs. So I've never told anyone about Lila except for an acquaintance of mine who has also gone through this. What's more, the social forces which push black males towards jail or early death are so much harder to fight than others will ever understand. I can imagine some asshole reading this book and saying "maybe he DID do something terrible." And I, as a black man can only watch the dominoes fall accordingly. There is an extra-legal, socially suggested presumption of guilt among non-blacks that only a fleet of EEGs and MRIs can convince you is there—even among those who say they don't see color. And while the brain scans can clearly show our prejudiced reactions, and the text miners can clearly extract our racially biased text even when we can't, we still deny it, claiming to be "cautious" or "logical." How easy it is to lynch somebody with a mind sopped in rationality; nobody knows a witch hunt until he's been a witch himself.

Now I ask you, if a man finds himself accused of something he didn't do, and he can't respond with trained masculine reactions because they'll make him look like he did it, and he can't just stay quiet because the rumor train will only get worse if he does, what kinds of options does he have? Only non-macho ones. Hopefully he's comfortable using them.

#MeToo

The mere hint of impropriety can destroy a man decades later if the wrong person he may have once offended suddenly sees him rising in public and decides his progress should be stopped. Not necessarily because he committed any offense back then, but because she doesn't like what she sees right now. This is not a statement of any specific case, but a statement of how, in some situations, the accusations really are false. Relatedly, while trends like #MeToo provide a valuable unmasking of various levels of abuses levied upon women, the basic training we males receive for being forward, bold, and honest with the women we like presents us with lines so blurry that they are often impossible to see, let alone walk. As easy as it is for a woman to find a #MeToo event in her history, it is equally easy for a man to have his tone and message transformed into an event he never intended. What strikes someone as harmlessly charming (or at least amusingly awkward) 9 times out of 10 can be permanently registered as punishable sexual-ish harassment the 10th time, and the man may never know anything happened until years later.

> *Apologize for what?* Some accused men will invariably say. *I don't even know what I did. It would have been nice if she had told me so I could stop whatever it was.* Going back in time he thinks to himself, *Believe me I'm not trying to get investigated 20 years from now over this normal exchange I'm having with you. If there's something about it that bothers you then for God's sake let me know! WTF, man. Putting a time bomb on this thing is not right!*

Based on what I've seen, he probably wasn't trying to rob her of power or self-respect. It may actually have been the exact opposite. He just wanted to complement her in line with his male impulse. Yet fanned by our American megaphone to wildfire levels, the collective effect of being a man instantly placed into the Monster's Club leaves no room for apologies, discussion, clarification, or anything. Just scared bosses and terminations, broadcasted shaming and demonization, a poisoned grapevine, and—in extreme cases—legal troubles.

Unfortunately for our society as a whole, we have yet to distinguish between #MeToo-Acknowledge the Event, #MeToo-Punish Him, and #MeToo-Empower Me. So the effect of the movement as a whole seems to promise all three results for every identified man's case by mass association. Although I suspect most people speaking up are more interested in reclaiming their power and dignity than in punishing the accused, the punishment for the latter is automatic. And although I know many people who would say "he probably deserved the punishment for being rude, reckless or stupid," we don't know that. Just imagine your brother, husband, son, or some other male you care about having a #MeToo claim placed on him by four or five people from somewhere in his past whom he thought he was simply being nice to. Imagine him being dragged through the mud with you over a thing that may or may not have been as significant as the collective inertia is bound to make it out to be. I understand the merits of a movement like this, and the causes for speaking up will truly exist for the majority, but still…Tied to a *collective trend*, the grains can build a mountain. As a male you just wish people would ask more questions before they donate their voices towards your hanging. Despite my identification with feminism, you might see why I—along with many any other males who've ever been demonized for innocent acts—won't warm as easily to something as widely sprayed and destructive to us as this. Without any policy or two-way dialogue behind it, all we get is a vast terrain littered with social land mines.

I don't expect many die hard women's rights advocates to agree with my assessment of #MeToo. I'm just telling you what it does to men. You can't have a society which trains a man to be the hot, charming guy who sweeps her off her feet only to get hunted down by a mob for doing so. As with Black Lives Matter and Occupy, #MeToo raises awareness, but hurts reconciliation. It also alienates those on the other side who would otherwise work with you to solve the issues, because they're too busy fortifying their class membership against your team's next raid. Movements like this need discussion to go with them, not just declarations and pointed fingers.

When you're a black male you worry about things that generate mass anger at your class even more, because you know that American society can be extraordinarily caustic and excessively ugly when it thinks you're guilty of something. The false stories have happened to a handful of good men I know (more of them black) though

all males face this. And they've happened to me on a
more minor scale on the mouths of rumor mongers.
There, all you can do is hope that you get a jury—legal or
figurative—which actually asks deep questions. In the
case of Lila and me in largely not-black San Antonio, I
couldn't assume this. Her refusal to tell *me* "It's okay. I
just my regular sadness. It's not you" was a cruelty far
worse than cheating or fighting with me.

So we ended it

Back to my story, over the next couple of months I tried to
tell Lila I loved her twice, partly because I meant it and
partly so that she would talk to me about what she was
feeling. But I got nothing. So I eventually texted her and
ended our friendship "suddenly" after eight years. But it
wasn't really that sudden was it? As with other
exchanges, non-communication killed me and Lila. She
was the only person who ever seriously broke my heart.
Afterwards I would cave in and finally buy a book I had
been eyeing for a while: Elizabeth Abbott's *History of
Celibacy.*[4] Given the stories it contained of reclaimed
personal power and of certain great people's refusal to be
distracted by their bodily desires, I fully embraced
non-sexual polyamory and avoided sex for the next three
years. Lila was the last time. Barring a deep kind of trust,
a cheap orgasm comes at an immeasurably high price for
one who absolutely must defend his psychological space

from girls with mysterious motives. So I chose to build up my own personal power in place of some random relationship with some random woman whose aims weren't confirmed to match mine.

You might find it ironic then, that ever since I've adopted an aversion to most formal commitments, I've flirted more, been happier, been more comfortable with myself, achieved more of my personal goals, and generally established much better relationships with women. A few of my past exchanges would still tell you I was either creepy by manner or a jerk by attitude, but I've found that the girls who do this all have one thing in common: They've all been selfish to the point of empowering themselves at the man's expense rather than by the man's side, and they all have relationship pasts which affirm this. That is, they've damaged other people's lives—male or female—besides yours. Apparently it's a common third wave problem—a kind of insatiable consumerism when it comes to social validation. Not that these women were bad people. Frankly, they were simply stronger willed than other women I've known. The cost, though, is that these kinds of women really will steamroll you if you don't actively defend your right to define yourself as their guy. For non-black women, it also helps if you're not-black. Or rich.

And so I've often found myself taking up the feminist position in my relationships with patriarchally trained women. "I know society has made you think you can tell me how to be a better male, but you don't have to listen to yourself. And I can't disrespect you the way you disrespect me. I can't cut you down the way you cut me down." She is that woman, and I am the one who's not allowed to resist her cage without risking any number of social repercussions. Lila was an accidental example of this, but I'm sure male readers have run into plenty of partners who've cornered them like this on purpose. As a male you learn to steer clear of malicious types like that and hang around more understanding women instead. The other ones can *stay* lonely.

On non-standard relationships

Throughout my "do not engage" phase with girls, an expanded circle of female friends, connections with enterprising women, and a more free-spirited tolerance for others' non-hetero lifestyles (especially towards the BDSM community), have truly made me a better person. Like a certain subset of Doms, I've gained a strong sense of discipline and personal power from being able to influence others without being dragged into their darkness, and gained a much higher respect for people who dare to share intimacy in ways that actually match them rather than ways scripted by the very judgmental heteronormative Western world. I've studied all kinds of fetishes, found some that I like, and more importantly, learned why those fetishes appeal to me. Once a person graduates past *Fifty Shades* in their BDSM education, I highly suggest they check out the actual lifestyle if for no other reason than the deep psychological insight it offers. You'll learn tons about communication and consent, respect for a partner's boundaries, attention to a partner's unique approaches to pleasure and, in some cases, of the skeletons in your own mind which cause you to gravitate towards the practices that you gravitate towards.

Thanks largely to my investigations of BDSM, I learned that I am polyamorous—one who loves more than one person at a time, though not necessarily sexually. That is, I'm a poly who doesn't swing. Why did I evolve to thrive in these kinds of multi-partner relationships? Partly because my early programming as a caretaker for <u>two</u> brothers trained me to frame happiness in terms of the "absence of exclusion"—seeing one partner in harmonious exchange with another partner who's not me. This also explains why all of my stable relationships have revolved around shared work for the community much more than on our interaction with each other as individuals.

I learned that monogamy for me is both a state of slavery as well as one of overcommitment foisted on one partner by the other. I learned that, as a scholar, I like to see situations from a third person perspective—not as a voyeur, but as a pattern-solver—so that one-on-one sex frustrates my ability to observe the other person fully. I don't like first person sex any more than I like first person shooters (video games), because the whole thing makes me feel perceptually claustrophobic. For me, bonded trios have always been better whether in the bed or out. Also, trios give me the all-important opportunity to observe Partner A's response to Partner B who is not me, so the chances of faking, failing, or getting trapped in something (personally) awkward are noticeably lower. Watching my girl get pleased by another girl is a thing of true beauty. But even if A and B never meet, the mere fact that I always let them know about each other means that I get to see both in circumstances *not* tied to their interaction with me. So it's a lot easier to spot when either of the relationships is going wrong. You'll find this out once you try it.

Oh, and one last note on poly: You don't always have to request a formal "open relationship" to set up a polyamorous dynamic for yourself. If you're okay with close platonic exchanges, and if you're sincere, all you need to do is allow yourself to love one person deeply.

Then love another deeply, with neither of them monopolizing your affections completely. It's not necessarily about formalizing the commitments, but it is all about how you choose to treat your favored people.

As a poly, I date less and commit less, but have LOTS more great bonds with various benefits. Even better, I'm not owned by any bad, selfish, or insecure mistresses. If chatting with a girl naturally raises the subject of relationships, I tell them I'm poly around the same time I tell them I don't want children. If they're turned off by either my stance on poly or on children, then I know they might be into a model of relationships incompatible with mine, and we may or may not take the conversation any further. For some men, the committed relationships may spell the death of freedom, where she can scold, cling to old flames, and hang out to her heart's content while he is punished for doing the same. But I deserve a two-way relationship. And so do you.

Where modern society has subjected many of us males to women with masculinized emasculating tactics we can do little about, we can see the problems of patriarchy ironically turned back upon us. Why should you as a male consider feminism? Because for some of us, the women who partner with us have been trained to use shoot-first assertion to own us—not because it's good for the exchange—but because macho is all any of us have ever known. Other, more considered forms of relating need equal air time; if we don't push for this, then we'll be pushed by pressures bigger than our partner alone. Although polyamory may seem soft-hearted because it's so heavily rooted in love and communication, many men will find it among the best routes to freedom from a single (often selfish) partners' tyranny. We love people in different ways—family, first loves, and fiery flings—and for me it's unreasonable to ask my partner to magically forget all of that if it's a part of who they are. But no one has the right to require that of me either. And I refuse to put my identity as a male in the hands of some bullying girl and her templates for how men ought to act. There are richer relationships beyond her, man. You *don't* need to convince her that you should both have rights to screw whomever. You just need to claim—if only for yourself—your own right to connect to anyone you connect to. But if she really is the only one in the world for you then that's also OK.

On non-standard sexuality

Now if you think fetishes are nasty, I'm pretty sure it's because you haven't tried any. Or maybe you've never actually looked at a full-scale list of fetishes. Do yourself a favor. Go grab your partner and look up a list. Just look at it together. Be awed. Share a good laugh. Be

flabbergasted together. But dude *get educated*. There are
so many hundreds of fetishes out there that a person
saying they're gross is a lot like saying every word in the
dictionary is gross. As with any behavior, specialized
sexual practices reflect the specialized psychologies of
those who engage them, and are no more unusual than
oral is from missionary. They can be as harmless as a
thing for high heels or as exotic as…well…they do get
pretty extravagant. Relatedly, I am only going to describe
my favorite corners of BDSM to you because it is
strongly related to my psychology and, accordingly, my
feminism. I'll also do it to help more conservative readers
get a sample of certain novelties and how they connect to
our preferences for basic thinking—like picking a
favorite zoo animal. You'll see how the practice matches
the outlook, so you and your partner might "unrepress"
certain truer forms of intimacy on your own:

- I relate easily to Daddy Doms. Not because I like
  control in real life (though I do), but because
  there are few things can turn me on like a great
  sub. Also, the idea of me being a sub myself
  makes no sense to me in any world. (Daddies
  differ from, say, Owners and Tamers in how they
  prefer to relate to their subs, though it's common
  to mix types in one person.)

② A Male Becoming Feminist

- Smoke and breath play addresses my desire for sophistication in the woman and strong dependency of one partner on another for the former's definition.

- Kigurumi and, relatedly, certain kinds of toys and machines address my emphasis on maximal pleasure for one partner without either partner putting on a fake face or feeling like a failure for not meeting the heteronormative template. Kigurumi is where at least one partner (or the sole participant) dresses up in something like a doll, anime, or a mascot suit, often completely obscuring their identity. The anonymity does wonders for certain kinds of personalities resistant to the over-gestured, often goofy bullshit of standard porn. The doll suits of kigurumi are, for me, a satire upon the scripted fakery of certain heteronormative dynamics. Also, the kigurumi I've experienced tends to be one thing that an American fuck buddy is often not: quiet. As in daily life, sometimes it's just nice to have a partner who knows how to shut the hell up. But if you do have a partner who bullies you into pounding it hard all the time, try putting a cartoon head on them. You'll smile more, I guarantee it.

As for machines, I already know myself. Given a choice to 1) set myself up for another epic failure with a woman I don't trust enough or 2) simply use a wand, I'd rather use the wand. If nothing else, it just seems better at its job than I am. (It also doesn't get depressed if it fails.)

- Latex emphasizes the curves of the body, full-contact sensuality (which appeals to a die-hard toucher like me), and again brings anonymity in cases where full body suits are used.

And speaking of epic failures, even though sex for me has not always been bad, my single-partnered relationships really have mostly ended badly. Partly because of my need for control, and partly because I'm attracted to women on the fringe who've been known to mess up peoples' lives anyway (both their own and others'). For this and other weird reasons which I hint at somewhere in my other books, I more or less dislike having orgasm in all but the most particular scenarios. Orgasm with the wrong person feels like I've taken a needed piece of myself and burned it. And sex, for me, is mostly work not play. Conversely, uncovering patterns for me is mostly like play, not work. Before I adopted celibacy, there were certain women who didn't evoke this feeling, but most

women did. So I don't miss intercourse, and have plenty
of less costly options for replacing it.

As for celibacy, for now it fits me. If I find someone I
trust, though, that can change. In her book Elizabeth
Abbott describes how certain abstainers considered it a
mark of defeat to finally have orgasm after years of
avoiding it. To each his own, I suppose. I think sex and
orgasm are natural though, and should be approached
fluidly by most people. To try to put the man before the
animal in this case seems unnecessarily difficult. To me,
extremes of non-expression seem just as undesirable as
extreme expression.

And why do you need to know all this? Finally we
come to the central connection of male sexuality to
feminism:

Judith Butler was right on when she argued for gender as
a performance gesture developed through habits. Such
habits can not only play a pivotal role in how (or if) we
get recognized as people, but also in how (or if) we can
survive as identities.[5] A man who is a man in the outside
world easily becomes another man's bitch behind bars. A
man who is a man to his subordinates easily becomes a
son to his mother. Thinking about sex and gender in terms
of power dynamics, we can see how a lot of what makes
you macho or dainty depends on what template you're

measuring yourself against. The story of my last days
with Lila and subsequent explorations of BDSM were
meant to serve a point; masculinity and femininity are
about much more than bodies, much more than power
versus receptiveness. Instead, masculinity and femininity
change form depending on where you are in a relationship
and even what you're doing. Who's on top, who's
vulnerable to whom, and who defines whose world can
change. Had she been a different kind of woman, Lila
could have fabricated all kinds of stories which really
could have ruined my life. But Lila's not a liar. People
may see Kigurumi as weird, and in the company of a
standard heteronormative group a person may be
ostracized by the "normal people" for liking it. Even
though that fetish may be closer to his actual psychology
than plain ole' boning. But again this is a matter of
behavior against a standard. Apparently it's more
acceptable to see real-looking people having fake fun
than fake-looking people having real fun.

Identifying as poly and connecting with the BDSM
community greatly increased my awareness of
heteronormative politics and the extent to which it clouds
our notions of masculinity and femininity. Somewhere
over the course of one's evolution as a man, actual
masculinity stops being important and a kind of
femininity disguised as masculinity takes over. Where the

importance of being a caring father, a loyal and serving husband, or an accomplished professional kicks in, the push for men to get along through *submission* to their interactants replaces the push for those men to dominate or define those interactants. As it is with actual hormones like estrogen and testosterone, even the most masculine men are socialized in 90% masculine-typical, 10% feminine-typical dynamics. Going beyond this renders him socially maladjusted as he attempts to run his family, for example, the way he runs his business. Control his wife the way he controls his subordinates at work? That would be seen as crazy. Yet in matters of sexual and romantic relationships, some men are quick to call other men weak for, say, failing to holler when the latter sees a girl he likes. Black men like my kind do this all the time. No one asks whether an attempt to pick up that woman is even a good idea. We just know that if she looks good on the surface and we all agree on this, making moves on her should automatically be one very real option. Considering the consequence first isn't celebrated here. Ironically though, conceding to the peer pressure *is* celebrated. "Submit to the peer pressure. Go be macho. (Without listening to her other cues first.)" Funny how we call things masculine when it's convenient for us, though they're actually not. (Like caving into the pressure to talk to a girl you REALLY don't want. To spare you the endless trouble ahead, you'd better pray to God that she turns you down.)

The point is, a man's real knowledge of his own psychology may lead him to embrace practices which lead him far from the masculine template handed to him. He could be embarrassed or shamed for it, but he doesn't have to be. Somewhere out there is another person who gets it. They tend to be much easier to find once you stop lying to yourself.

Summary

The terrain for classic manly men is littered with land mines. Even if you are the manliest, best-looking, richest, pro-athlete out there, you live in a world where normal people spreading normal gossip—with normal expectations—can render you a demon overnight should you fail to behave as advised. Holding the image of an ideal male is one thing. Possessing the respect for an ideal self is another. Some men have both, but many don't. We all have unique backstories which strongly push us towards certain traits that may or may not fit with the pressured template placed upon men, and some of us may face challenges when the traits that don't fit are left subject to assessment by others who don't care about the details. In cases where we seek out ways of relating that fulfill us, we often give others the right to judge us into a corner—the roles of good father, boyfriend, co-earner, and lover all handed down man-style by our favorite women and our favorite social institutions. If you are a male and you don't face this problem then good for you. That doesn't mean however that things are all good. In personal and public matters, we 21st century Westerners continue to operate under a shoot-first framework which privileges blind action over dialogue, so that the freedom to seek better ways are often limited because those better ways are not tough-looking enough. But what good is it to be tough if all you do is live to fight your own ally again tomorrow? One day we'll see these kinds of "hated love" connections for the self-degradation they really bring; until then all we have are our personal histories to tell us what works.

In this chapter I've talked about the chain of experiences that brought me closer to feminism—essentially by way of several non-macho, non-heteronormative roles that I've not only held but actually claimed proudly. I'm sure you've heard it before. In order to have genuinely good relationships with others you should really have a good relationship with yourself. If all we men consist of are bundles of masculinity and nothing else, then many of the places where we would do better to back off—like the family, marriage, or the negotiating table—simply won't be in our tool set. Feminism isn't just about women. It's about assertive versus receptive power dynamics. Somewhere in your history you may have found that receptiveness suits you better. Or maybe it suits your partner better. Either way, a world where the masculine and the feminine don't get equal air time is a world where even the most feminine-seeming associations of yours may only have masculine tactics for cornering you. Maybe you know this already. It can definitely be a problem. Accordingly, it's in our interest as men to support equality of power modes not for the sake of biological females, but for the sake our own psychological selves.

3. A Chapter for Black Males (Which Everyone Should Read)

When I'm not doing studying society and power relations, I have the good fortune of being an astrologer. Contrary to what many of us Americans are taught to think, doing astrology in an age where most of the people around you don't believe in astrology presents many hidden advantages for your understanding of relationships. Instead of looking at people as people, astrology chops those people up into packages of character: The ego, the form of influence, the type of self-advertising, the type of limits one tends to look at...Each of these is summarized by a planet, an angle, or a sign. Now that we have computers, the kinds of sociological knowledge we can get from classifying people in this way is boundless. Among the findings uncovered in my own work was a trio of asteroids which showed up frequently in the charts of black people and those with heavy black influences in their lives. These were Proserpina, Briseis, and Etheridgea. Proserpina in particular not only proved critical to my understanding of what it means to be black, but also contributed to my full conversion to feminism. Let me explain:

In order to find out what an unknown asteroid does in astrology, you do the same thing you do with any mysterious variable in statistics. You look at it among a group of factors you know and see where it's associated with the most change there. Proserpina popped up in Black charts, but when I looked at it in non-black charts, I found something interesting. The asteroid was associated with the agitation (or excitement) of the people *around* you, not really with you yourself. So if you had, say, the planet of conversation next to Proserpina, you were more likely to converse comfortably with black people, converse in a provocative way, or (most likely) rile up people more easily with your conversation even if you weren't being provocative. The finding blew my mind, and gave me an entirely new perspective on the both the black box and the male box.

For us black men, all our lives we are taught that sports and entertainment is the default route, jail comes more easily whether or not it's earned. The price for crimes is higher. The anger at OJs and Cosbys and *entire* Middle Eastern countries is exponentially higher than the anger at McVeighs, Zimmermans, Las Vegas or Columbine shooters. We demonize the former, mourn the victims or "investigate the motivations" of the latter. You know this is true. The security threat response is normal when we first encounter people outside of our color, and the social positions populated by us are almost always lower. That's in the outer world. For blacks specifically on an internal-cultural level, we're more boisterous, more lusty, less tolerant of our own connecting with other groups, and less likely to be accepted as leaders without that extra dose of criticality that a White or Asian person wouldn't get. Naturally then, we see ourselves as worth less societally, but stronger in our will to have value anyway. And why not? Whether in the US or China, Japan or France, darker skinned people all over the world need to offset random scorn somehow. But Proserpina's association with other people's reactions revealed even more.

I'll never forget being in eighth grade watching the split screen during the original OJ verdict. Broadly summarized, Black people cheered; White people were angry. And in the years since then it's still incredibly easy to make a non-black person angry by mentioning any major legal issue involving a notable black male. From OJ to Cosby to Obama you ask, "What is it that *I* did to warrant this kind of ugly reaction from this person? What is it that the famous person did to make witnesses' reactions not just angry, but hateful?" Now here's the surprise: In cases like that, it really is <u>the other person's</u> reaction to some topic on THEIR mind. Although everyone has been guilty of provoking something at one time or another, events we "provoke" partly through association with a particular look really are rooted in how society trained the one doing the looking. Not necessarily us being looked at.

Every trait of every kind has both a positive and a negative side depending on whether the person accessing that trait is comfortable accessing it. The accessor isn't always us. In public, the accessor is that public. So even though sports and entertainment seem (superficially) to be all we have, those outlets are part of a bigger effect which darker people have on lighter people all over the world: for better or worse, dark people excite others easily. It helps us scare and threaten others, but also impress others more easily whenever we do the same socially-favored thing that lighter people do. A black person walking into an upper-middle class store often threatens the people there more easily, putting them on alert. But a black leader who represents everyone (not just black causes) has an easier time charging up a crowd. A black scientist becomes "articulate" and is easily and proudly recommended to others (whether or not this is the result of "talking monkey" syndrome). As exciters of others, we find a socially safe place on the court or playing field. Except when we don't kneel to the flag. Then we excite people the other way—like any criminal or defendant presumed to be criminal. And because the

people who judge us through preprogrammed bias don't
know they're doing it, many swear on ten Bibles that they
are only assessing us "logically" as they would any other.
But when they *had* the chance to assess an equivalent
white perpetrator in the same way during last week's
news, they didn't. Is it institutionalized racism? I don't
think so. It is prejudice? Probably subconsciously, yes.
But that prejudice works in our favor IF we own the
favorable sides of our look's effect on others.

I like to think of our physical look as the package of
reactions we draw from others. Some of this package
we're free to modify, some of it we're stuck with. For the
parts we're stuck with, it's our two-fold task to surround
ourselves with people who accept those parts AND to
make sure those people are going where we want to go.
For darker people in any unequal society, that second part
is especially important, because otherwise it's easier for
us to keep the company of people who are just as
devalued as we are. You don't become a nigga unless you
hang around other niggaz to remind yourself of who you
are. Not that we Blacks should abandon our own. Just that
we should know: All over the world, to be darker-skinned
is to rile others up; sometimes, a riled up human damages
perfectly good opportunities. If the company we keep is
our own kind, we need to make sure that the ways in

which *we* get riled up around them are of the impressive type rather than the damaging type.

VERY generally, we observe lighter people setting the social rules in their respective societies all around the world. Again, for better or worse. Darker people excite others within those societies. For better or worse. This doesn't mean that darker people can't lead—only that, in unequal societies, we're not expected to. We *are* expected to do things and take up positions lower than the social standard. On the other side, lighter people aren't forbidden from being fun or "hip"—it's just that society is more surprised and more impressed when they excite us on the level we are taught to expect of our regular rappers and basketball players. To be a member of your ethnic-looking group is to present others with some basic assumptions. This is where choosing a road that fits with the rest of our identities is most important.

As animals, we humans are wired to draw quick conclusions about the foreign things we perceive. It aids our survival. Growing into a rough framework for how our own home cultures differ from the cultures of others, we hold stereotypes about those others as a kind of summary of what to expect from them. Although it's true that stereotypes applied against us can make us angry, such stereotypes are more a measure of the person's unfamiliarity with our class' look rather than any inherent need to discriminate against us individually. Actively discriminating against others takes work. Passively judging others based on what we've heard about their type…that's automatic.

Especially for members of lower-treated classes in an unequal society, an understanding of prejudice can greatly help us to escape social confinement; if someone else has what we want, arguing at that someone probably won't help us even if that other person really does treat us like shit. Does that make sense? If it doesn't make sense then try reversing positions. If you had a kind of status that someone else wanted, and that someone constantly complained about how you were denying them, would you give it to them? Because they are only one of an entire class or group of people doing the same thing, there's no possibility of shutting them up even if you gave it. So would you give them the status they whined for? I wouldn't. And probably couldn't. By the nature of what it means to be chronically dissatisfied as a group, no single compensating act will address their actual problem: the outlook which they hold. It's for this reason that—no matter how dissatisfied a group of women, a group of Blacks, a group of Occupy protesters, or a group of pro-lifers are—people who protest against the very groups who hold a monopoly on the influence sought, don't usually succeed. You want what The Man has, but your devisiveness only annoys him. And even though it isn't very fair to have negative stereotypes applied to you by people who don't know you—even less fair that you get punished for calling them out on it—stereotypes are THE thing that human brains fall back on when they don't have any more information about an experience in general. Red signs on the road make us hungry. Classical music seems refined. The Midwestern US seems "country." Stereotypes and (relatedly) cognitive heuristics are a basic part of animal thinking. Does that make negative stereotyping okay? Maybe not to everyone. But in the eyes of the person who thinks her interests may be compromised by your presence, it's just common sense self-defense. To fight them on this is to attack them just as they knew you would. So they defend even more. Ours is not to push them around to make them okay with us. Our task is to become okay with how our class might be broadly seen in general, then build our other, better traits on top of it.

I've talked about the American stereotyping of certain groups a previous book. So here I'll broadly summarize only the most salient qualities of some American classes:

- Lighter-skinned people set the social standard, but can be oblivious to occasions when they've devalued others

- Darker-skinned people more easily excite others around them, but can also agitate or threaten them in the process

- Whites are associated with the norms of communication: visual, spoken, traded (as in money) or otherwise

- Blacks are associated with the norms for charging people up, in whatever situation this might play out

- Hispanics are associated with the norms of family, peer alliances and in-group focus, not just privately but on the level of nations

- Asians are associated with the norms of tradition, generational alliances, and focus on the institutions that steer one's behavior

- Native Americans are associated with the norms of association with natural phenomena

- Middle Easterners are associated with the norms of community control and the exotic ideas that come with this

Those are some basic groupings. We often run into people who deny equality to those from outside their home class. But the home class is only part of the formula for class mobility. Careers, styles of one-on-one communication, identity labels, and the friends we choose each make a major difference in how strangers piece together their opinions of us with the home class in mind. For example, I'm black but identify partly as (and usually speak to people) like a Buddhist. Strangers tend to behave funny around me until I start talking to them, and then they usually try to be much nicer. A man can be ghetto as hell, but if he knows a little about history and can match the 2010s with the 1920s in conversation then certain kinds of opportunities will open for him. The point is, it's not solely about being black, but about where you display it. In the absence of other information, a generic Black amongst generic Hispanics will have different expectations put on him than a generic Black among generic Asians. If he doesn't value those expectations enough to adhere to them, but keeps striving for the rewards those groups hold, he can expect difficulty. Hopefully you can see what I mean here. Blacks who

want White money but don't like White people may have
to get that money somewhere else.

While we're on the subject of group values, I've run into
many upward-moving Hispanic women in San Antonio
who only accept White or light-skinned males as the ideal
partner. This might make sense if you think of the array of
stereotypes involved, but as we saw above, what
constitutes an ideal depends on what you're after.
Because the US is obsessed with money and status,
Whites, blondes, "hot" guys, sexy brunettes, and career
business people are all examples of the gold standard for
other groups whose classes aren't so celebrated. Not only
are we taught that we need money in order to survive, but
we're also taught that we need *a lot* of money for it. Most
of us know, however, that beyond what we need to live
reasonably comfortably, that second part isn't usually
true even if the first part is true enough. Looking at the
American dream only through the lens of retirement
funds may work for some, but it's not the only lens. If
happy family relations are more important to you past a
certain amount of money, you may see a more family
centric-class as your gold standard. If it's a sense of
excitement you seek, you may see a more excitable class
as your gold standard. Because I'm big on community
and exotic ideas, I have a soft spot for Middle Eastern
women (though all women are great). I also love

philosophy and complex ideas, and gravitate towards Czech and Russian ways of thinking. Every class has its appeal, but we shouldn't be surprised if the person with the microphone tells us that having the microphone brings the best life of all. Of course, if you don't know yourself that well, the trained gold standard is all you'll have.

Consistently I've observed that people who seek the trained gold standard—with a passion that makes them inclined to disrespect all others—are fundamentally bitter or insecure as individuals. That's no exaggeration, only what I've seen personally. Perhaps this is a byproduct of forcing oneself to stick with her prejudices even when doing so is destructive or unnatural in her many other relationships. She forces herself to devalue family-focus, devalue the power to excite, devalue group legacy, or devalue whatever else so that she can have that status in the eyes of others. For the men out there who've dealt with this kind of thing, it's rarely useful to partner with someone who breaks everything except for 1) her perfect ideal and 2) the followers who serve at her convenience. A woman who sees the worst in all other things will probably see the worst in you eventually. Often she feels she must do this in order to avoid seeing the worst in herself. As with the disempowered protesters I mentioned earlier, it may not be worth it for you to try fixing a problem rooted deep in her attitude. It will only contaminate your own attitude. Don't let a bitter critic tell you how to meet her personal standards when she can't even meet her own. That's what I've learned.

To be Black is to charge up the behavior of witnesses by default. Combine your power to charge others up with any of your other personal talents and you'll see that being black isn't nearly as bad as American life has taught us to think. For other ethnic-looking groups there are other automatic effects. If we want the right to be our full selves without shame, the first thing we need to do is own our public effects on purpose. To reclaim our legitimacy as men, we need to see the physical look we'll always carry with us for the asset that it is, then invest that asset in the right groups of allies.

4. Black Male Feminist

Now in case I haven't said it yet, I love being black. I love being male. I have all kinds of habits that would make a more straight-laced person cringe. I still say nigga, dawg, and (believe it or not) homey. I drop F-bombs, MF-bombs, and—despite being celibate—still have a pretty fierce appetite for T&A. If I think a girl is sexy I tell her so (as long as it's not rude), and display a quirky collection of disruptive behaviors in a group. Not because I'm a delinquent or because society told me, but because it's natural. As a thoroughly self-confident male, I don't believe that the passion for life that I bring should be bottled in by people who only know how to cage themselves. When I die, no one's going to say "that Mike was so well-behaved in that meeting." But a few people who really buy what I'm selling will say "I once knew this dude who lived life all the way up to its limit. Even in places without rules to guide him." That's the shoot-first side of masculinity. As a biological male who is also a scholar, I like being able to go places and not have people fuck with me if I don't want 'em to. And because I like so many unusual and sometimes feminine things, I LOVE being able to instantly turn a situation around if anyone thinks it's okay to disrespect where I stand. Even as a "nerd," I was never bullied in school. Male. Black. Plus I can put on a convincingly mean look which, to this day, can threaten most people enough to clear out unwanted pressures. These are some of the advantages of being who I am. You have advantages too. Own 'em. As males we are expected to use that shoot-first approach to situations, and so are less likely to face impediments when we want to do something in new territory. I want to convince the reader that owning his position as a male is key to attaining wants that are his own rather than wants handed to him by society, his job, or his partner alone. Once he's really owned himself, he may start to notice something.

I became a feminist in earnest once I realized that some of the women I had been partnered with were more determined to measure their womanhood against their ability to fight a man than they were in simply being good people. In the current age of third wave girl power, there's this tendency for some women—especially middle class and lower—to build relationships upon a kind of sassy, belligerent disrespect of the man they're associated with. As I described earlier, these women—though pretty mean to all but the most ideal friends—were also very strong. And so am I. Thus it took me a while to notice my own pattern of partnering with difficult women only to enter a power struggle with them. I said to myself,

- *If only she could simply listen or talk things out instead of doing all this...*

- *If only she didn't just put up walls when someone truly in her corner tried to relate smoothly...*

- *Despite her stereotypes for my look and her need to flatter herself at my expense, it's not always about her pussy; sometimes a brotha really just wants to get a simple job done...*

Since my calm negotiation only invited more tyranny on her part (in more than one exchange), I realized that what we had was a general non-respect for ways of relating that weren't bullying and masculine. *If I were a white male she'd be all on my nuts instead. She said so herself. We'd be fucking instead of fighting. But when she does get her ideal male, she commandeers his life with her validation needs. And here she is. A woman trained by macho men to think that the best way to maintain a partnership with a strong male is to be either a perfect wife or a bitch. With nothing in between. Sharing power—rather than warring for it—is of course out of the question.* These are actual thoughts that I had. And sometimes I really would share these thoughts with the woman in question. Cuz I really am male; whether she's offended or not, sometimes I really don't give a shit anymore.

Still, in my mind, macho patriarchy is as damaging to the partnerships we form than it is to the individuals within those partnerships. If anything goes wrong, all we have are the missiles. If we disagree, we head straight for the troops (i.e. family and cliques). While I was coming to terms with this pattern of relationship formation with difficult women, I was also developing great relationships with other women who were more spiritual, more empowered, more creative, and much more cooperative. The business that one of the difficult partners and I worked on accidentally evolved a mostly female target market, and the types of allies I gained in the process were essentially feminine. As a member of an "underclass" I gravitated towards research on dehumanization, interpersonal relationships, and power abuse as a way of understanding the framework of devaluation some of my former partners had tried to foist upon the exchange. And without knowing it, most of my work aimed at balancing power dynamics became work strongly associated with women's voices. Not as victims, but as identity shapers against an outside world drunk on jobs, economy, and socially-recommended templates.

Like being polyamorous or an oldest brother, feminism isn't something that I had a lifelong wish to embrace. I was (and am still) a male who doesn't like having his expression confined by other people's shoot-first imposition. As I've undertaken work to eliminate those confinements in my own life, I've landed in a circle of people who strive to eliminate expressive confinements broadly. These are mostly women with something to say and contributions to make in a society flooded beneath a billion noisy assertions. Surely you've experienced the rampant opinion-spitting via the most intrusively masculinized media tools available. It's not the voices that bully us; it's the broad culture of posted insistence which carries those voices. We all talk too much. We listen much less. So when you begin actively promoting listening and cooperation as real ideas, you may end up closer to the definitions of second and fourth wave feminism than you expected. That's what happened to me.

A thing at its maximum turns into its opposite. For those of us males fortunate to become confident enough in our male sides, we learn that it isn't necessary to box every person who throws rocks at us. Some of us just want peace sometimes. And we take up activities that balance such peace with a comfortable level of assertion. Although I'm writing this book, I'm mainly writing it for men as a way of letting them know that we don't have to be provoked into chaos by the various pressuring forces out there. I'm not writing it to convince any particular group of women that I'm a genuine feminist. I don't care about that. To me, the actions we take in work, relationships, the enterprises we take on, and how we use power on others speak louder than rebellious-sounding words dumped out from a single biology.

Males as feminists in practice

What does a male need to do in order to practice feminism? In an ironic turn of equality, you might say that all he needs to do is call himself a feminist and be intense when he does it. That's a good enough standard for a female to be seen as one isn't it? She doesn't actually have to contribute to research and policy, participate in discussions or anything like that? Of course I'm being facetious. But maybe you can see how it might not make sense to ask questions like this if we're not willing to truly examine our own notions of equality. If a male and a female both claim feminism and perform the same acts in the process, then to say that the male is less genuine because he doesn't have a vagina could be seen (by some) as a type of discrimination.

Realistically though, I truly don't believe that a man simply claiming feminism should have the same weight as a woman claiming it. Not only has he not lived the experience of womanhood and it's 20% representation in the US congress,[6] with its pay gap[7] and predisposition towards objectification[8]; not only does he not have to deal with the same kinds of abuse, societal pressures for self-worth, motherhood, and goal validation;[9] but he also has to somehow pretend past the advantage he has in being able to drop his commitment to it whenever he feels like it. A woman can't just stop being a woman and go back to her male privileges, but a man can. Proving herself in the ring full of masculine types will always be a potential part of her job. This is the biggest problem we run into in defining feminism in terms of male and female biology. The two sides will NEVER be equal. Not in any practical way (barring some revolutionary technology which changes this on a global scale).

Looking at feminism in terms of biologies only makes matters worse. Biology based, "women's club" feminism ignores all of the important nuances of masculine and feminine relationships focused on in the second wave. Now that the body can vote, how about respecting the behavior? And we extend this to many other areas of human relations.

Policy, prejudice, gender, self-image, etc… As long as feminism is thought of as a woman-only cause, not only will males be disallowed from supporting it actively, women will be capped in progress related to any matters beyond the biological, because those interactions rooted in non-exclusively biological differences will be deemphasized as things to address (such as maternity leave, abortion rights, and women in combat). These are issues which combine biology with other topics, but if biology remains the central dividing line for what constitutes a feminist, more nuanced topics like these will be harder to discuss and address. As a society we already know this. Even though we as citizens still automatically associate feminism with women only, it has officially—publicly— been about much more than that at least since the time of Simone de Beauvoir's[10] writings in the 1940s and 1950s. Women yes. Women-only, no.

In a different turn, expanding feminism into to larger realm of "feminine" (not just "woman") things, the barrier to male entry into the cause becomes lower. No longer are feminists merely thought of as a club of women who want what we have but who won't let us into their meetings. It's now all about shoot-first versus process-first dynamics. Male feminists are distinguished by the extent to which they put their money where their mouth is in advancing equal air time for those aspects of our lives that encompass the full array of process-first dynamics. This includes our assumptions about social roles typically reserved for women. Whether it's writing about the issues to increase our understanding, sponsoring groups to air important issues, or simply supporting policy efforts, anyone can support any cause, but the feminist cause is more practically served by males doing things like this. Black causes are more practically served by non-Blacks doing things like this. And why would a male waste his time with causes of this nature? Because if he's like me (as described in the previous chapter), his identity might be anchored to far too many "non-masculine" roles—far too many roles for which patriarchal heteronormativity would punish him—to simply sit around and let everyone else's machismo drive his whole world into the ground. If he's to ever regain his respect as a nurturing parent, a servant to others, a possessor of dreams beyond his wife's, or as a spiritual person, he can't afford to let simply patriarchy shame him for valuing these. He has the right—and the social means—to defend other things besides his license to carry a gun.

When people ask me what makes me feminist, I usually give a shorter answer than the one above: I've unintentionally grown into a person who thinks the world would be better with less asshole behavior on the part of everyone. Like a classic aggressive human male, I tend to dislike other assertive males in my space. Almost all of my friends are female (because they listen and think instead of asserting their damned ego points all the time), and almost all of my work is of the kind that revolves around power subjects, with a hefty distrust of Western scientific empiricism—especially as an astrologer. So I like to do my research without necessarily having the dick-wagging rules of academia lord over me all the time. Whether in conversation, the rules of science, politics, or the social consequences of being a colored person in the US, I've found that male stuff is full of shit if not appropriately balanced. And you too will discover this the more you tap into your own proudly male sides. The day you get to that point where you realize that no other dude (or no other girlfriend acting like a dude) is really tolerable as a puppetmaster anymore, you'll say to yourself, *These people's testosteronic shenanigans ain't where it's at.* On that day you may consider the real importance of actively supporting a more equal way of relating—if for no other reason than for the sake of better, more meaningful company for yourself.

5. A Short Note on Feminism's Four Waves

So that we all might be equally informed before proceeding, let's review American feminism's basic stages. As of the early 21st century, American feminism has consisted of three waves plus one:

- The **first wave** focused on **I. achieving voting rights** (Woman Suffrage) officially beginning with Elizabeth Cady Stanton's call at Seneca Falls in 1848[11] and ending in 1920 when President Woodrow Wilson signed the women's vote into law after World War I.[12] During the War women had shown that they truly could do the jobs of those men who had been away on the front lines, only to be forced to give those jobs back up after the men returned home. This was unacceptable. Over the two years following the end of WWI in 1918, the call for suffrage had only gotten louder. Thus the vote was finally granted.

- Feminism's **second wave** occurred alongside the
  Civil Rights Movement and Vietnam War
  protests, as people all over the US without an
  equal voice demanded to be heard AND taken
  seriously. Specifically, the center of the second
  wave read, **"II. Don't treat me like a piece of
  meat**." In the decades following suffrage in 1920,
  women had seen how the vote was not enough,
  when most of the people allowed into the good
  ole boy system were still, of course, good ole
  boys. "Father knows best" said the country. "Stay
  in the kitchen while we do real man things" said
  the country. "We are men. You are Other," it
  said.[13] It was during the second wave that the
  famous bra burning and protest groups came into
  being. Perhaps more importantly for us today, the
  second wave was also when feminist scholars
  began to define how overly masculine ways of
  thinking—in academics, in psychology,[14] and in
  politics for example—held everyone back.[15]
  Leave it to the patriarchy to prolong a war with
  which so many disagreed, use violence against its
  own citizens, and to degrade them by *defining*
  them as naturally worth less politically.

- As Vietnam came to a close and the Civil Rights
  Act of 1964 began to take root, the essential

cause of traditionally underprivileged groups had finally been addressed via a major law. The act forbade discrimination on the basis of race, color, religion, sex or national origin, so that the US' chief engine of social progress—industry— could no longer use shadow methods to keep the old barriers in place. From here, underprivileged groups would evolve systems to help them "catch up" where they had been previously denied, bringing us to the age of Affirmative Action[16] in the employment system, and "**III. Girl Power**" in the popular American culture.

- For me, popular **third wave feminism** begins in earnest with Madonna and the cone bra of 1990. Although the actual third wave had been in effect for several years as international feminist scholars questioned the American-centric, exclusionary interests of the movement,[17] it wasn't until we saw Madonna reverse power roles that the message of the third wave truly began to hit us: "You're still treating us like objects? Okay, we'll use that objectification as a source of power." Since then, the images of the strong woman, equipped with all assets— physical, intellectual, professional, and confidence-wise—have become commonplace in the media, pulling many areas of social and cultural reality with it. Women have seen marked improvements in social status, respect, and partial independence from men's ways of thinking as the third wave mantra of Girl Power has taken the strengths of the woman to new heights. And yet there remain problems...I'll get back to those shortly.

- There is a growing evolution into a **fourth wave** of feminism which focuses more on the communicative and psychological aspects of the feminist message—especially applied to social issues. If the third wave has been all about Girl Power, the fourth Wave is all about equal social voices.[18] Issues of human trafficking, body stigma, queer and transgender rights, and a general defiance of traditional heteronormative boxes lie at the core of the rising fourth wave—which might be best described as "**IV. Social Empowerment Beyond Heteronormativity**."[19] This is the first time that same-sex and transgender rights have played a major role in the feminist cause. It also differs greatly from the third wave in its emphasis on the right to own one's own body—in whatever way one means this.

Now I argue that most Americans aren't actually experiencing a fourth wave world. We're stuck in a darker side of the third wave: Sex as a weapon. That is, current American society advertises cone bras and sass for all girls, political power and irreverence—guns and contracts—for all guys. Although the fourth wave cause is certainly a promising continuation of second-wave ideals, the US overall hasn't gotten past the more visual body-commoditization of the third wave. When Beyoncé tells you she's an independent woman, that only the strong survive, and when a generation of young girls follow her lead, her record label and the industry powers that be—still overwhelmingly male—forget to tell you that her message of "sexy independent womanhood" is still heavily owned and operated by manhood. In my book, Beyoncé remains one of the key positive symbols of third wave feminism as well as one of the more unfortunate examples of its dark side: the side that makes it seem as if men are of no value in this empowerment picture, though men continue to hold plenty value in writing what that empowerment picture looks like. And how far it's allowed to go.

Third wave girl-power is good. Third wave trampling of boy-power is not good, especially if boys still hold many of the important cards. In the same way that the existence of BET (Black Entertainment Television) without equal acceptability of a "WET" ensures that we blacks will never integrate past a certain point, existing social standards which insult the male's worth but tiptoe around the female's continued unequal treatment ensures that women will retain lower overall worth than men in the change-making positions that truly matter. If we all know how important men are in legislating the context of equality, but bury that importance under masculinized impositions of girl-power without equivalent images of proper manhood, we get a society frustrated with pictures that don't match reality. This is as true of race as it is for sex.

As a male who actually watches the old westerns *Gunsmoke* and *Rifleman*—who remembers Christopher Reeves as Superman and Operation Desert Storm, I still have some idea of what a responsible, balanced masculine figure or leadership action looks like. Our 21st century commercials are full of flippant dumbasses. Our girl-power girls strongly celebrate guys as props for their own esteem. As for the real men we all know who are still working jobs and navigating the society that devalues their real-world efforts? They're not interesting enough. I argue that the third wave has pushed a lot of necessary man-training into the background, but that lack of training in male role-models has only made us dissonant as a society.

And so we have the emerging fourth wave, where people other than women are finally beginning to benefit from the expressive advances developed in the previous waves. The challenge for us men is to integrate the new fourth wave thinking into our family and social structures—especially as a way of offsetting the more negative side effects of an age ripe for the frustration of manhood. One of those major side effects occurs when the society-wide devaluation of a man's worth is brought to a boil, culminating in violence against others.

6. On Abuse and Domestic Violence

One of the goals of fourth wave feminism is to call attention to the areas in which exploitation and abuse are simply accepted as an insidious fact—lightly addressed while normal society goes about its normal socially-pasteurized business. From human trafficking to domestic violence to emotional abuse, there are major social issues we are aware of but not committed enough to seek solutions to through voting or formal advocacy. One of the central problems with addressing society's various forms of abuse is that we have not yet developed two key corners of the lens for viewing it. These are the class lens and the perpetrator lens. With a stronger focus primarily on the abuse of individuals rather than on the abuse of groups—with a stronger focus on the perspective of the victim rather than the factors that create perpetrators, we've remained restricted to looking at only one third of the problem.[20] In order to take abuse seriously, an entire society needs a consistent conception of what it is. Then that society needs a decent understanding of *why* it is. Why is it that many of our friends and neighbors who were by all rights normal in other areas, may grow dangerous and damaging through a select, gradual turn of events? Reminding the reader that I am writing this book primarily for males, I'll spend this chapter talking about how we see abuse differently; then we'll use that different perspective to create better circumstances for ourselves and others around us.

As a male in the early 21st century US, you know the deal: When people talk about abusers, they're usually talking about your kind. You're encouraged to put on your political correctness hat; even if you're not required to apologize for all men, you're greatly discouraged from showing various forms of energetic disagreement with the person doing the talking. You know that it is unacceptable to mention those times that you've personally experienced where she really did start it—even if your point is just to say that it may not have been 100% the man's fault. And you're usually encouraged to assign fault to him. In her case, you might get away with blaming a rough childhood or social training or other pressures she's facing. But this typically doesn't fly for men. You know the deal. As a male, you're inclined to be pulled into most discussions about abuse with most of your proper dialoguing powers taken away. And here's the irony:

Suppose some friends of mine are talking the troubles experienced by a married couple we know. It's obvious there is some emotional abuse going on. We also know that there has been violence once or twice. We've heard that he's controlling. She's miserable, and yet she stays. Some of my friends wonder why they don't just get a divorce, and have talked to the woman about seeking help. Yet nothing changes. Suppose this is the scenario.

Do you think I should do anything about this situation?

Would you?

Even if you—like most of us Westerners—think it's none of our business, do you think I should _say_ anything about this situation?

> To him?

> To her?

> To the police?

> To my friends?

I'm male, remember. My guess is that, although you wouldn't expect me to intervene or say anything to the couple, you *would* expect me to chime in with my own

response to *you*, the gossiper. Ultimately I do, and here's
what my response sounds like:

> "Man, that sucks. She should get help."

And how does that response fix anything? It probably
doesn't, but at least I've done my part as a
sympathetic-sounding conversation partner.

The problem with situations like the above is that I have
no real options for doing anything. I usually can't say
things like

> "Maybe she's done stuff too. Remember when
> she did that [fill in the blank]?"

I'd be "blaming the victim." What's more, I can't say
things like

> "Maybe she *is* a victim, but of what? How do we
> know what goes on in that house and whether
> he's also a victim?"

I'd be thought insensitive. Worst of all, I can't usually say
things like

> "Maybe someone should help *him*."

Not without serious justification. The irony of all this is
that any attempt by me to put together the other side of

that situation is, by social suggestion, shut down before it gets off the ground. So all we have are one-sided monster stories. And the missiles that come with them. Recall that whole system of non-collaboration we saw earlier. This was where our taking a finger pointing, masculine-favored stance prevents real solutions from being presented; when it comes to the subject of abuse, we are expected to be outraged more than we are expected to sit down and work out something better. I believe this is one of the strongest examples of where the advocate's use of masculine dialoguing harms the very aims of advocacy. If you've ever tried to solve a two-sided problem by framing both sides in terms of only one, then you know the result is usually continued disagreement, a stalemate, an unhappy loser and a winner who'll need to fight the same fight again tomorrow. Issues of abuse don't just live in the framework of the victim. They also live in the motivations of the perpetrator.

As a younger man I passed through one or two occasions where I really was angry enough to kill. Both objects were male, but I've also been angry enough with one particular woman to want to ruin her life through a series of calculated actions. Those cases were well over a decade ago, but they made obvious to me something that may not be obvious to a lot of vocal anti-abuse advocates:

⑥ On Abuse & Domestic Violence

Why do men actively abuse others tied to them?
Often because they subconsciously see
themselves as having run out of options.

You say I need to be a man. You scold. You
criticize. You compare me to some ideal which I
can never be. Your family and friends make it a
point to shame me for not providing you with
enough of whatever it is they expect you to get
from your man. I need to respect your
independent womanhood but when I go out and
do the kinds of "independent" things you do,
you're jealous. You say I need to make more
money, but I can't just go out and apply for that
menial job without giving up my self-respect.
Still I tried and tried, and they *still* didn't hire me.
I'm not rich enough. I haven't been a good
enough provider. I don't satisfy you the way I did
when we were still dating and our connection was
new. And I have all these goddamn people in my
ear insisting be superman. Even as I struggle, all
you do is bitch. Our conversations are always
about what I need to do for you and the kids and
everybody else, but never about how you can
help me help you. It seems like all of society is
constantly on my case, challenging me to "be
somebody" in everyone's eyes. Yet no one cares

that I work hard unless we're slapping loads of travel pics for their approval on Instagram. If I turn my eye towards a hot girl, I'm a demon. If I need a break from you, I'm a lazy jerk. And I had insecurities too before we met. But I'm obligated to help you through yours while keeping up the manly front that mine don't exist. Every man on TV is clean, pretty, rich, and provides great sex all day. And your social-noise training has you thinking that I should just take the unending assault on any pride of accomplishment I might have. Fuck you.

See all that? That's why men abuse a little. From there they are cited as demons, stripped of key social support for getting them out of the coming cycle. Then they abuse a lot. Maybe some people won't like that explanation, preferring to blindly lynch the accused instead. But we should ask whether those people have actually personally helped reduce the number of abusers with that war-like attitude. Or have they just been loud and mad?

Now, nobody's saying that abuse is okay. But for anyone interested in knowing, this is how it happens. "He's just a defective monster" is NOT an explanation we can build effective solutions on any more than "She's just a victim" is. And *somebody* needs to talk honestly about the world full of factors that sap a man's pride, effectively putting him in a corner where options are concerned.[21]

In cases where I can't show my frustration in public without risking termination or jail, ostracism, or public shaming, I turn to her—the one I'm already fighting with anyway. Starting with unkind words, we graduate towards purposeful emotional hurt, retaliation, things that make the other person jealous, then onto things that intentionally make the other person feel less powerful. After emotional hurt we move onto hurt of the psychological kind, but if we're ever mad enough to destroy real things in each other's company, or angry enough to seek an instant, silencing stop to what's going on, violence—for some—may be the end point.

The current popular conception of domestic violence focuses on the victim—as it probably should. But perhaps you can see how a man driven to commit violence by factors such as those above might see this as a giant pity party being thrown for a person who has added more than her fair share to the situation. A society aimed at "getting her away from that monster," aimed at outside parties breaking what we're both inclined to hold together, aimed at "*them* correcting him"—is not one you'd expect to reduce the number of abusers. Even with a small number physical abusers locked up, we end up with emotional abusers who know not to get out of line publicly, psychological abusers who employ various behavioral tactics for diminishing the worth of the partner beyond the relationship, or (in a case that many of us will be familiar with) dads and boyfriends who just walk out. And what about her? If her natural dynamic is to fight—because masculinized passion is what she knows—then we have two people whose problems aren't really solved even if there IS outside intervention.

So what's the solution to all of this? Clearly it's not the kind that can just happen overnight, but I will propose one later in this chapter. Before that, let's look at the other part of the lens for understanding abuse: that of the societal level.

In the US we tend to believe strongly in self-determination. The kind of not-in-my-backyard philosophy is alive and well such that, for classes not our own, we easily respond with a combination of sympathetic conversation and pull-yourself-up-by-your-bootstraps logic which makes us okay with the misfortune of groups who don't sit where we sit. This holds for socioeconomic status, ethnicity, disability, gender, and any number of classes for which there is a distinguishing physical or behavioral feature. So when someone tells us about the continued impoverishment of many Native

American groups our reply is "Man that sucks. They should get help." Human trafficking? "Man that sucks." Some kind of local disaster? Depending on the area and the *social importance* of the population, "Man that sucks." So New York is a big deal while Puerto Rico and Louisiana are not. The exception to this kind of bystander effect occurs in groups which either share our ideal identity or groups which make us feel superior. It's easier to feel really bad and donate real money after looking at sad animals with the ASPCA than it is to bother getting educated about transgender rights. There are boundaries of social acceptability and the line of taboo certainly, but the idea is that, on a collective level, we don't really see instances of mass abuse as such unless it appeals to our individual-centric sentiments. So our heuristics for knowing how to respond to issues like domestic violence remain partly informed by our training in society-wide equivalents. Unless it involves immediate threat to ourselves, those near us, or those like us, or those we aspire to be, the default isn't just to do nothing, but to armchair it to each other as a way of making that nothing look like something. So we have a lot of amplifying statistics and tweeted rage, but not a lot of concerted education on the issues and even less policy. Not surprisingly, it is safer for us to have an intense *opinion* regarding domestic violence than it is to get actively involved in the way we would with, say, a random local singles meetup. Before you take this as a criticism of society, though, there's something important we should address.

I've found that, in general, most of us are well intentioned. We would do something to help others

1) if it fit within efforts we knew how to donate,
2) if we thought we would make a difference,
3) if it didn't impose a burden on the lives we've already set up, and
4) if we knew more about how the specific issue affected us.

It's truly not reasonable to join every crusade out there, and it's not clear that certain issues such as human trafficking even affect most of us in any immediately meaningful way. But I've argued throughout these chapters that feminist issues are everyone's issues—starting primarily with the need for additional forms of social and interpersonal problem solving. It may not be the case that Arizona's prison complex means anything to you; it may not even strike you that the system of social imbalances that support that complex are meaningfully related to the corporation-controlled lobbies keeping you living paycheck-to-paycheck until you die; but one thing may occur to you more immediately than anything else: people and systems alike are more inclined to exploit others when the exploiters run out of better options. Whether it's a political system that won't get fixed or a family situation spiraling ever downward, it's not enough to look at the victims and once again tell ourselves how much that sucks. In exploitation systems, the victims typically have far less overt power than the perpetrators do. And although few victims are truly powerless, much of the potential solution in an exploitation system lies in the realm of the perpetrator. If we don't ask who the perpetrators are, what creates them, or even determine whether or not they're actually perpetrators, then we won't have a the tools for real solutions—just outraged people spraying their rage into a mixed crowd.

To address the other side of issues like domestic violence and other systems of exploitation, we need more programs which reopen alternative options for all involved. We can curse that "abusive" monster all day, but if we haven't asked whether our facts about the situation are even accurate, if we're more interested in yakking about it than improving it, if our solution is to tear up whatever it is that keeps the abuser and the victim together without regard to where either will go after the relationship breaks, our system of one-sided conflict management will only release two broken parties into the wild instead of one. So congratulations to you; you've helped reinforce something she already knew. What now? The kids? Her self-worth? Do you think the monster story about him will be enough for her to build her own worth on?

Even having never been part of an abusive relationship, I can tell you that most kinds of separations built on other-demonizing don't produce better escapees nearly as much as you think. You still have to deal with the remaining bitterness and the resentment among other things.

As men, the best thing we can do for ourselves—the action which will ultimately have the biggest positive effect on broader society—is to recover our sense of pride. To be the best man I can be, to find that niche where my biologically mandated shoot-first side is at full peak, is to find within myself a characteristic which no company, clique, or girlfriend can take away. The solution to abuse and exploitation on levels public and private is for us to regain the side of ourselves which is immune to misleading pressures. Where we would otherwise be frustrated by a society that values only perfection, we each need to find that area of life where we are unashamedly male—powerful enough to naturally plant our flag in places far beyond ourselves.

Not only should we reestablish the basis for our self-respect, we eventually need to apply that basis for the benefit of others beyond us. The logic of this is simple. If you are, say, an expert in making people laugh, carrying your expertise with you serves to offset any claims by the outside world that your worth should be circumscribed by its template. You have a talent which few on the template can match, because most people aren't funny. Not only might you possibly use this talent to make a place for yourself in the paying world, you might also use it to enhance the lives of others broadly.

The benefit of using a talent which is uniquely your own is severalfold: Any claims by others that you *haven't tried hard enough* or *haven't made your mark* will stop making sense to you; you won't be so willing to settle for partners and employers who chop you down, because you'll recognize them as being full of shit; lastly, you'll build a bigger circle of people who actually like what you have to offer. If you're invested enough in the man you uncover, you'll be a lot less likely to get embroiled in battles defending a man who isn't there.

As for the issue of abuse, there are plenty of advocacy agencies and passionate people who will eventually have their day at a publicly hailed, welcoming policy table. At that table, those pushing to end the exploitation of others on all levels will encounter men like us—trained to be tough, but empowered enough to contribute that strength to the build-up of the systems for which we are partly responsible. There, we'll be too busy moving the world around us to be bothered by the little minds that harass us—the empty media images that excite our women but don't pay our bills. Society has taught you to respect her, but you need to respect yourself too—wherever that leads you. Don't let the world you're in rob you of the man you were meant to be.

This is the age of girl power. Many of our fathers couldn't cope well enough to teach us how to handle it. So we've tried to be who the world has continually challenged us (and taunted us) to be, only to be shamed for not being all things to all people. But the Western world itself doesn't seem to be a very happy one, so what the hell does it know? For those who have made mistakes carving out our manhood in a world that doesn't seem to appreciate it, you're not alone. Look in the mirror. Look at the thing you are strongest at providing. If necessary, forgive yourself for not tapping into it sooner. Then start again, as we men are trained to do.

We should note that as you get better, you may find plenty of people—plenty of world—reminding you of how you used to be "worthless." You can do whatever you want

with those relationships that drag you backwards, but
know that you don't actually need to stand for this.

It's okay to do what you have to AND do what you want
to at the same time. If anyone says it isn't so, you might
want to find someone more supportive of your strength.
No one should be forced to stay stuck in an environment
which brings out the caged animal in him. For a better
world, for better relationships to that world, we need to be
better men—not by following the patriarchal template or
the preaching of everyone with an opinion, but by
following our strengths. With more of us beneficially
affecting the larger circles around us, the inclination to
mistreat others in defense of our weaker selves will surely
lose its appeal.

Let's summarize this.

**To fight against abuse out there, we men need to
recover our self-respect in here.**

**The things that drive us to abuse are the things that
take our options away**: our pride, our ability to respond,
control of our work, fair and equal dealings with our
partners, the ability to ignore who the commercials and
social gossip say we "should be," or the right to have
non-standard interests without someone else giving their
bullshit opinion of it. And then again, sometimes it's just

our partner abusing us with ongoing jabs at who we are.
Or who we're NOT.

**If our society as a whole is insensitive to abuse on a
group level, we shouldn't be surprised if we're limited
to responding to it on a personal level**. To look down on
Mexicans or transgender folks is to help yourself look
down on anyone whose characteristics remind you of
those groups—even yourself. (You won't see it until your
subconscious comes back to bite you later.) If you
associate Mexicans with group solidarity and hard work,
but look down on them for example, you may find
yourself punishing yourself for what you see as having to
lean on others even as you do the best you can. If you look
down on transgender people, you may be much more
easily shamed, self-denying, or generally angry when that
better-looking male actually does things you like better
than you do; jealousy will more easily make you a hater,
and an ineffective one at that.

**Even if you have no interest in abuse advocacy, surely
you yourself don't like being tread on** by certain people
and their close-mindedness, the double standards for men
in scandal, the number of women who you're sure
became managers at 21 because they were pretty, the
number of times you couldn't call a bitch out even though
she acted like one (though she can call you a dick as many

times as she wants). Maybe you don't care about the empowered running guiltlessly over the disempowered. But when *you're* disempowered by society itself, maybe the idea of "the strong conquering the weak" won't sit so well with you after all. As a man in the 21st century US, you're probably in a weakened negotiating position much more than you realize. IF, that is, you're still holding on to the old ways of underestimating the people and grapevine around you. Little people in big positions—or tiny people with grand voices—can mess up your world pretty quickly. Either build that fairness for everyone around you, big or small, or watch your own unfairness get thrown back in your face time and again. You know it's true.

Lastly (and this may be hard for many to accept), know that anyone can become the abuser if caged long enough. Anyone can become a victim if restricted enough in the choices they perceive. It may not be your thing to actively go out and push for anti-abuse causes, but a poor-victim/perpetrator-as-monster perspective will only go so far in gaining the general support of the often accused male class. **Accused perpetrators aren't always guilty, but even guilty perpetrators have reasons. Ignoring those reasons only cages them more, and makes solutions for all parties harder to *present* (let alone apply)**. That's fine if you don't plan to see the perpetrator again. But if you or the victim *will* need to see the perpetrator again…well…you know.

> Also, ignoring the perpetrator's reasons prevents us from positively influencing future perpetrators like them. And why would we want to do that? Because the future perpetrator in this case hasn't perpetrated yet. Anyone—even you—can be a "future" perpetrator if we put you in a situation where the inner animal is all you have to rely on. So behavioral modification isn't what we want, is it? Monster stories are a bad foundation for change. **Positive empowerment beforehand is the goal**—especially for a society full of males who haven't had a healthy <u>culture</u> of masculine role models since the cartoons of the early 1980s.
>
> *Onesies and twosies aren't enough.*
>
> *Mafioso badasses don't match most of our daily lives.*
>
> *Angsty superheroes put their own skeletons before the greater good.*
>
> *Reality TV fills us with the expectation of viral smiles and cutesy irreverence 24-7.*

Images of caring fathers without images of fathers who know how to healthily discipline their children leave us stuck with a culture of mothers only—strong within the family bounds but only half-prepared for the chaotic world beyond those bounds. `Devaluing the male/father = a compromised toolset in the child for actions-first even amidst uncertainty`[22]*—mostly with respect to groups outside of the familiar circle of favorite... everything.*[23] *No wonder we lean on super-Presidents, mega-companies, and feel-better drugs to pick up the slack for us.*

Now if you as a male really want to do anything to help that couple in which the man is said to be a monster (and if you're on good enough terms with that accused abuser), maybe the best thing you can do is—without diving into the couple's business—help the male get his pride back. Don't lecture him. Don't correct him. Don't put him in the same corner that you wouldn't want to be put in if you had the same frustrations. In other words, don't take more of the power he's already lost—the same loss which likely helped cause the situation in the first place. Just be a good enough man to show everyone (including your opinion-spitting peers and girlfriend) that the fully equipped route—the route with access to both masculine and feminine tactics—might be easier than the rage train. And if ending an abusive relationship really is the best thing, whether that relationship is yours or someone else's, consider ending it as painlessly as possible—in a way that will preserve your self-respect when you look back later on how you chose to act. Hopefully your decision will have been a real one, NOT just another armchair tweet from a uselessly angry gossiper.

7. One Man's Understanding of Sex, Gender, and Feminism

With one of the heavier topics aside, let's build up some more nuanced frameworks. The writings on feminism are vast and complex, spanning over two centuries of perspectives on equality. Since I couldn't hope to condense it here, I'll just present some layman's ideas of what feminism and what its technical pieces are all about.

I'll warn you ahead of time that you'll need to be okay with gray areas, paradoxes, or whatever before proceeding, because it's going to sound like I'm saying two different things at once. To get around this potential area of confusion, just think about how power works in your own relationships. In some ways you have more; in other ways *they* have more; in still other ways, you have more again. Look at it this way and you'll be alright.

How a male might view his feminist partner

One very basic definition of feminism is "the advocacy of women's rights on the grounds of the equality of the sexes."[24] I guess I can kind of live with that. But not really. When I as a male am in an active romantic relationship with you (my woman)—listening to you and doing things for you, it is easy for me to see the sexes as plenty equal. You can tell me about unequal pay, unequal political voice, and unequal access to power, and I'll probably hear you. However, within our immediate societal context, the practical reality for me is that I'll probably see myself, not you, as defining the boundaries of our exchange in the outside world. That is, I'll basically see myself as the stronger in the social possession sense no matter how much pull you have over me within the relationship or within our local peer groups. You, on the other hand, will lean more on your friends and your emotions to determine your interaction with me. This is how I'll typically see it as a male in a normal heterosexual relationship: I'm tougher, you're more emotion-driven. There are major consequences for this kind of generalization, though.

As a male in a relationship with you, the woman, my basic assumption of being "stronger" than you (in whatever way that applies) means that regardless of what you tell me about women's rights in the world, there will be a part of me which—on the immediate personal level—thinks of you as weaker (or at least less strong) by design. Biological or social design. Our biological differences will only compound this, because on average you really will be shorter or smaller than me, you really will be more collectivist in your friendship groups— "leaning on others" as it were—and you really will be the one who issues the commands while I'll be the one who carries them out. So when you remind me that women out there aren't treated equally, I remind myself that the woman in here isn't really entitled to more "equality" than she already has. My interaction with you is more real than my interaction with that unequal world outside. So your claim of inequality, no matter how valid it may be, simply won't take with me. Our own dynamics with each other will render everything else moot.

When we talk about feminism as pushing equality of the sexes, we end up with two problems: First, it isn't clear what is meant by equality. Equality out there or equality between us? I just talked about this. And of course they're not the same. The unfortunate reality is that "equality between us" is much more likely to override "equality out there" simply because it's more immediate to me. Under these circumstances I'm less likely to support feminism beyond lip service because I already have my hands full keeping up with your template for my masculine performance within the relationship. But this is actually a standard for the animal kingdom.

In most species, the males compete with each other for female attention, and have evolved to be stronger in order to beat up other males. This is referred to as sexual selection.[25] Here, it's common that males fight each other, and females get their pick. It is far less common that females fight each other or that males get their pick from the pool of possible mates. Now given that modern human culture has produced an extremely competitive field where females compete to impress others via the standards of beauty, and given that reality TV would have you think that a lot of the mating game involves females competing for a guy or his status, you might think that basic sexual selection doesn't apply to humans. But it does.[26] Reality TV makes good TV because it's different from the boring reality we know: the one where girls really don't have to do much to get a guy to fall for them. The whole "competition to be beautiful" isn't nearly as natural to human women as "*male promotion* of women's competition to be beautiful *so that the strongest, highest status males can select from the most attractive, highest status females*." This societally imposed competition benefits high status males and females at the expense of everyone else. The point is, equality is tough to achieve here because the balance between the group encouraged to compete on strength and a second group encouraged to select from the first group, is unequal. Biology and evolution really do make us unequal, and this is borne out in the basic differences between how men and women look physically. No, this doesn't mean that biology promotes *social* inequality. It means that biology promotes (typically obvious) *physical* inequality. But I'm sure you knew that. The problem is, much like the race issue, when we start using physical differences to determine social superiority and inferiority, biological differences are used to *justify* social differences, so that in my subconsciously trained male mind, your compressed male-feminist discussion sounds like this:

Female: We need equal rights in the world.

Male: I know.

Female: I want to do something a about it.

Male: Cool, like what?

Female: Like raise awareness or something.

Male: Cool.

Female: Aren't you going to support me?

Male: Sure. You have my support.

Female: No, I mean support me with action.

Male: I already do that on the personal level.

Female: No, I mean support me *out there*.

Male: Nope.

Female: Why not?

Male: Look at you, being emotional over something that doesn't immediately affect me or us. Going to your friends in a bigger scale version of girl-talk. If you really deserved strength and power on the world stage like men have, you would—

Female: [tapping impatiently]

Male: You would just pull yourselves up the way we do instead of meeting all the time. But I don't really see you doing that because you're, you know, girlier than people like me.

Female: So I don't deserve equal rights?

Male: You *have* equal rights and you have my moral support. What more do you want?

Female: I want you to respect or *actively* support my cause.

Male: By doing what? I'm just a man, so I can only relate so much. But I support you.

Female: ...

At least our man didn't bring up things like "you almost had a president" or "you have your own networks." The point is that, as social power holders, we men find it simpler to dismiss feminism when the issues are approached in terms of "equality." Before our eyes, men and women neither *look* the same nor *act* the same socially. As good of a definition as "equality of the sexes" might be, from a male perspective this clashes with the idea that men and women are fundamentally physically and behaviorally unequal. Don't expect a male to support feminism on the basis of traditional "equality." Generic equality automatically prompts us to think in terms of visible differences. Social inequality automatically prompts us to think of behavioral differences. With males evolved through fighting each other for superiority, and with males trained to assess others for physical weakness or threat level, an "equality" argument won't make sense to us past a certain point.

The second problem with defining feminism as pushing equality of the sexes lies in the definition of "sexes." I know; that refers to physical men and physical women right? But we should hope not. See the first problem for why using the term "sexes" eventually caps the reach of feminism. An appeal to something rooted in biological difference won't help us push towards equality. Of course there are nuances. Of course there is a much deeper meaning to the term "sexes." Those kinds of academic meanings are part of what drew me to feminism in the first place, and I'll even appeal to one in this chapter. But in general, policy makers and the common public won't look any deeper than womanhood and manhood when we use a term like "sexes" to describe what feminism is after. There has to be a term which discourages attention to known visible differences. Also, sex is easily confused with sexuality, and both are easily confused with gender. So when we say "equality of the sexes" not only do we have a definition which reminds us of visible differences in which men have the upper hand, we also have a definition in which the notion of one's "sex" is muddled. That's good for a certain level of inclusiveness, but bad for the crafting of targeted social policy. For example, if I'm a male politician who wants to restrict access to abortion, I can use "equality of the sexes" to advance an argument like this:

> "All people—men, women, and children—were created equal. Because of this—because I support equality of the sexes—I am voting to restrict funding to programs which subsidize abortion clinics. For the lives of all boys and girls who

would not have had a chance, my vote is a vote for equality for all."

This is the kind of argument I would encourage my pro-life students to advance during our political science debates. Regardless of where you stand on pro-life versus pro-choice, the above argument exploits vagueness in "equality of the sexes" to argue for equality in the extreme. That argument would be harder to make if we conceived of sex in term of power dynamics rather than physiology, and that's what I'll argue for shortly.

An alternative look at feminism

Honestly, I think defining feminism as "advancing equality of the sexes" is a great definition. One of the best on-paper definitions we can come up with. But real-world publics have their own ideas about what sex and equality mean. Those ideas fly in the face of the real qualities we judge in people right before our eyes. So let's come up with an alternate definition of feminism specifically designed to 1) gain both male and female support and 2) clarify what kind of equality we're seeking.

Feminism promotes the balance between (stereotyped) male and female approaches to problems.

Now I'll be honest with you. I don't like this definition. A part of me hates myself for saying we should use it. Below are some obvious problems with it:

- By "male" I actually mean "masculine-element." Male is biological. Masculine is behavioral. Masculine-element is relational—taking this whole dynamic and extending it to non-human ideas like design structures and business processes. The basic public, however, won't take the time to understand these differences. So we just say "male" because it's shorter.

- By "female" I actually mean feminine-element. As with maleness versus masculinity, these aren't the same.

- By "problems" I actually mean issues. Problems are things with definite solutions where there is basically a right and wrong. Issues are things with *approaches to solutions*, where there is no real right or wrong.[27] Framing problems (like that pothole in the street) tends to be a simple masculine finger-pointing task. Framing issues (like school vouchers) tends to involve more complex, feminine-element discussion, and can't usually be solved by simple labeling or sending troops somewhere.

- By "balance" I actually mean "equal air time appropriate to the situation." But the latter is too long for branding purposes.

Another problem with the above definition of feminism is that it de-emphasizes women as the focus. Some might even say that "feminism" is the wrong word. Maybe we should call it "humanist" or something. But I disagree. This is a semantic matter which could be a chapter in itself, but my two basic arguments for sticking with the word feminism go like this:

- Changing the word really does kill women as the focus of the definition. But the inequalities are still there, and striking a power balance remains favorable to women in a society where the *default* is imbalanced power in favor of men.

- Beginning at the biological level, men are encouraged to shoot first while women are encouraged to get shot at first (figuratively). If you put these two kinds of people in a room, the shoot-first group will typically set the agenda. An argument for balance means that first-shooters and second-shooters are somehow both first in terms of how and when they the get listened to. I won't call this unnatural, but I will argue that, again, this favors the second group's power more than it favors the first. In the short run. In the long run it favors everyone by diminishing the gap between first and second, enabling the firsts to ultimately go farther. Again this argument can get pretty deep, but I'm basically claiming that balance for men and women *is* power for women in the same way that balance between first turn-taker and second turn-taker *is* power for the second turn taker. Firstness versus secondness is, by definition, imbalanced. To put secondness on a level equal with firstness is to somehow defeat the whole point of firstness. As with picking two first place winners in a contest instead of just one, the pick who would have been second enjoys all the rights of firstness while the one who would have been first gets both the rank and any community perks that come with sharing the win. Surely you've experienced this.

Yet another major problem with my definition of feminism is that it encourages a certain level of chauvinism in males. "Okay, I won't send the missile. I'll listen to you for a little while with my 'FEMALE' side. Hahahahaha!" As a male I'll tell you that this kind of condescension *will* happen among those of us who use the above definition. However, I believe that the room for chauvinism is exactly what the definition of feminism

needs in order for real progress to be made on higher
political levels. We need a way for masculine males to
respect feminine approaches while still retaining their
toughness in the eyes of everyone else. That arrogant
asshole may joke about taking a FEMALE approach to
things, but if he actually *does* listen, collectivize, employ
participatory leadership, display introspection, or use his
common sense instead of leaning on authoritatively
declared citations alone, then he would have moved
towards the very balance we seek.

Whatever the case, we end up with an actual, technical
(fourth wave) definition of feminism which I as a male
can more easily support:

> **Feminism** (full definition) **promotes
> situation-appropriate air time for masculine- and
> feminine-element framing of issues, with an
> emphasis on reducing situation-*in*appropriate
> masculine-element bias.**

"Situation-appropriate" is our way of recognizing that
some cases really do call for heavy masculinity or heavy
femininity. Masculine-feminine biases are more natural
in martial and maternity matters; it would be generally
impractical to argue for total equality of approach in
these.

Differences in connotation

Feminism as "advancing a balance between male and female" is a definition that trades accuracy for practicality. It doesn't say what it means, but like a good folk story, it's better at making its point in the minds of those who hear it. When we pursue a balance between [masculine-element] and [feminine-element] approaches in addressing reproductive rights, for example, I think it becomes much clearer to all of us that more women should have a say in this. Feminism as "equality of the sexes"—by biological implication—doesn't imply this. Instead it conjures a kind of "They have babies, we don't. Oh well…" response.

When we pursue a "balance between [masculine-element] and [feminine-element] approaches" on the political representational level, I think it becomes clearer to us that 1/5 female representation in Congress in the land of the free is unacceptable. For me as a black male, having 4/5 of Congress continue to do as the country has always done isn't very useful. Instead of actively addressing the issues that plague "my kind," administration after administration attempts to respond to it with a one-shot regulatory crusade or a one-shot exercise of police powers. A one-shot speech or something. On this point, all three of the most recent US Presidential administrations have essentially used masculine tactics to steamroll the will of their opposition. The Bush Jr., Obama, and Trump eras have all done this, but I argue that this is less a reflection of them personally or as leaders and more a reflection of the kinds of tools our political system has to work with. If power subjects don't vote or aren't educated to vote responsibly, if they don't speak up while their children's schools yield to some funding-addicted police state or shiny-new-private-for-profit trend, it won't matter which daddy deploys which troops or where. Troops it is. (Even if they look like internally-directed regulators, as in President Obama's case). On issues like this, Medicare, social security, or guns, "equality of the sexes" means next to nothing. "Balanced [masculine] and [feminine] problem solving" goes beyond sex to immediately affect how <u>all</u> decisions are made.

Central ideas

It's about here that we should probably have definitions for all the moving parts involved in universalized feminism. First, let's define **universalized feminism** as **feminism defined in terms of the broad social interest, independent of individual identity.** Judith Butler's "gender as a performance gesture"[28] and Emi Koyama's Transfeminist Manifesto[29] both lend themselves to universalized feminist arguments to the extent that they frame gender as a function of changeable identity rather than a function of static categories. Static categories too often lead us back to the ultimate static categories of male-female biological difference. And that's where male support stops. It's hard for us to think of equality when the two sides involved are visibly unequal. But males still control much of the access to the kinds of systems women seek to influence. Where male institutional support stops, feminist institutional access faces a plateau. It may not stop entirely, but it will slow down noticeably. We've seen this already though in government and in business. Lots of girl power. Not a lot of girls *in* power (as in CEOs and the US Legislature).

And now for some basics:

Sex

Sex is a biological category for classifying you as male or female.

> **Male** is a biological category in humans evolved to favor **dominance over members of the same category (other males), the approval of members of its opposing category (female),** and the display of physical power or aggressive potential for advancing these ends.

> **Female** is a biological category in humans evolved to favor **the approval of members of the**

same category (other females), the dominance over members of its opposing category (male), and the display of physical attractiveness or protective potential for advancing these ends.

In other words, males dominate each other and cooperate with females. Females cooperate with each other and dominate males, and our bodies are designed to promote this. So says the average animal species at least.[30]

Each of these categories come from anthropology. How "male" is male? I don't know. But if we use definitions like the ones above, a person is more male to the extent that his biology fits the male description more strongly. A related notion of "femaleness" also applies.

Sexuality

We'll refer to **your combination of masculinity and femininity** as your **sexuality**. Given the following definitions, you'll see that a person <u>cannot</u> be 100% of any of these.

Masculinity is a pattern of behavior which comes with **a preference for the kinds of actions and responses that constitute a biological male**. In a body evolved for within-group dominance and out-group cooperation, you would expect certain things:

- Later evolved males will be **bigger and physically stronger-looking** than their earlier counterparts. Will they actually be stronger than their ape forebears? Probably not. For a stable society where we're not constantly tearing each other apart, we need to be able to win fights, but fight less. Threaten more, but follow through less.

- Later evolved males will need to be **ready to fight or show focused dominance behaviors** in the face of new things of uncertain threat level. Otherwise they die. So a central quality of masculinity is flag-planting, labeling, declaring, and otherwise insinuating yourself into things you know nothing about. Favorably in the eyes of others, we call this bravery or boldness. Inappropriately at the bar, girls call this creepy or stupid. (Mainly when it comes from guys they don't want, of course. Otherwise it becomes boldness again.) Dominance in the face of an unknown threat gives us the first/"actor" half of masculinity as an actor-receiver dynamic.

- Later evolved males, though **tasked to cooperate with females, will tend to take them less seriously once they've connected with those** females. Why? Because the uncertainty of lacking a bonded mate will be gone. Also, the female who ultimately accepted you poses less of a status threat to you than they did when you were courting them. So my ass stays planted on that couch unless something is on fire. Accordingly, our bodies also evolved to use feel good chemicals like oxytocin to reward ourselves for giving a damn.[31] Lessened threat after a mate has been secured gives us the second/"receiver" half of masculinity as an actor-receiver dynamic.

The second point sounds like some women you know, right? Yes. And it ends up raising a real issue in how we socialize males and females. But I've already talked about this in previous chapters.

Femininity is a pattern of behavior which comes with a preference for the kinds of actions and responses that constitute a biological female. In a body evolved for within-group cooperation and out-group dominance, we can expect the following:

- Later evolved females will appear less threatening to males than their earlier counterparts. Physical traits that deemphasize being ripped and ready to fight, and instead emphasize mothering, stability, and a lack of tension will be favored. So the breasts, hips, comparatively less-pronounced muscle tone, friendlier faces, and smoother body shapes are all more greatly favored. Even though males are evolved to develop desirability in the eyes of females, and even though females still get their pick, a female whose physical or overt behavioral features compete with a male's for dominance is less likely to be a female that a male cares to fight for in the first place. You're a human reader. You know this is true. There are implications here for how we have evolved certain standards of beauty across cultures.

- Later evolved females will display other, non-physical methods for dominating their mate. Male hormonal weakness helps this; female cooperation with other females is another; broad social status mechanisms are another.

- As a male concerned with protecting his personal power from females who don't match me, I sometimes think of certain women as being like a kind of terrorist attempting to weasel into my mental stadium. "Look, I'm unarmed. She says." But she's already captured my hormones, so I'm inclined to let her in. She also knows a bunch of other people in and around the stadium, so if I try to drop my seed and abandon her, that network will punish me. And if I'm attracted to her deeply enough, she'll surround my stadium with trophies of solid gold so that I can dedicate my dominance behaviors to pursuing them. All for her. Even after I obtain her hand, rather than allowing me to get lazy with her, she'll use other connections in my mental stadium, other golden trophies, and other non-threatening invitations to encourage me to do what she wants. At that rate, I'll never leave (even if my inner animal says I should). Is this just a story? Just me being paranoid? No, it's an analogy for the ways in which females benefit from mechanisms not directly tied to them to recruit male compliance. Males also have these mechanisms. But in females, their effective use is more important, since the appearance of direct threat in the eyes of a male won't win her nearly as many fans. Males are praised for such direct displays of dominance, and have less of a directive to seek power through systems beyond their individual effort. With typically socialized females, the dominance comes through the network.

The pressure to dominate a potential mate in various ways *after* he has appeared on the scene gives us the notion of femininity as a receiver-actor dynamic.

- Later evolved females will develop more extensive social mechanisms for cooperation with other females. As the pool of possible mates gets bigger, so too does the social support structure for sharing information across friendship networks. This is another area of scientific research which social media companies are well familiar with. One of the subfields is called Social Network Analysis.[32] But the bottom line is that social connectedness becomes more important as human females evolve. Again, this kind of thing is useful for males too, but not nearly as important for ensuring their individual successes.

So now we finally have a foundation for talking about masculinity versus femininity. Notice how we all use each of these tactics, not just the ones typical of our biology. So while masculinity and femininity definitely hold significance as power-related social concepts, "100% masculinity" or "100% femininity" doesn't serve any practical purpose other than ego posing.

In the above conception, <u>sexuality comprises basic behavioral patterns that look like *what we would expect* from respective male and female biologies</u>. But something big is missing here.

I'll bet you thought "sexuality" would include topics such as being straight or gay. But we haven't talked about other-preference yet. Isn't a masculine person supposed to prefer females? Isn't a feminine person supposed to prefer males? No and no. Not necessarily. There's enough research in biology and psychology to separate preference from identity, but we don't even need to go that far. If you just remind yourself of the standard butch-femme archetype, you know that sex, sexuality, and gender can all be separated. That said, let's talk about gender.

Gender

Gender describes **a person's preference for bonding with mates of a certain sex relative to their own**. It drives me nuts that most public institutions still use the word gender (preference) when they really mean sex (biology). But I guess I understand it. We're still squeamish about that kind of thing in the West, and no one wants to be the business that makes people giggle every time they see the "s" word.

> **Heterosexuality** is **a person's preference for mating with the "opposite" sex**.

Homosexuality is a person's preference for mating with the same sex.

Bisexuality is a person's preference for mating with either sex.

These are easy enough, but I actually had to think a little before settling on these. Why not "…mating with the same *sexuality*"? I decided that, to return to the butch-femme example, same- or opposite-sex**uality** doesn't really work for how we typically describe these kinds of pairings. Also, we just saw that sexuality is more like a "ratio" of masculinity to femininity while sex is a more fixed physical category. On the most basic level, we don't actually go out there and ask people how masculine or feminine they are in deciding whether they're viable mates. We just look at their physical sex and go from there.

Interestingly, under the above definitions, a person would be considered transgender not because they changed their *preferred* sex, but because they changed their *own* sex. So if I were to transition from male to female and people described me as transgender for it, the term might still apply even though my actual gender change (assuming I still preferred women) would have been from heterosexual to homosexual. It would not have been because I changed from male to female. Not to argue with

queer theorists and other experts on the matter.[33] This is
just the way you'd frame things if you used the above
definitions. **Transgender** changes gender (preferences
against one's own). **Transsexual** changes sex (some
aspects of biology).

Now I'll go out on a limb here and extend an existing
category to contain all of the other assorted preferences
which people have that don't register unless activated by
special events. These include types like sapiosexual
(being turned on by intellect) or demisexual (only being
turned on with a strong emotional connection). I'll file
these under "asexuality" since the default preference for
these people is no preference. But if we're dealing with a
demisexual or sapiosexual who tends to *prefer* being
turned on (as opposed to not preferring it), then these
types will fit better under bisexuality.

Asexuality is a person's preference for mating with
neither sex. Does anyone actually do this? Yes.
Though it's more of a psychobiological mandate than
a social leaning, unlike the other three.

If you think about it, the early animal in us really
shouldn't be expected to confine the reproductive impulse
to interactions evolved by the later animal. But it does
happen. So although people might scoff at terms like
demisexual, yes it is a real thing and no it doesn't apply to

everyone. Like so many other areas of identity, you don't appreciate things like this until the heteronormative world labels you dysfunctional for it.

One last word on gender. One of the ideas that I encountered frequently as a young black male is the argument that, if you're a man who has sex with a man, that automatically makes you gay. I never quite bought this idea, mainly because when girls go through what is known to be a fairly common experimental phase, it doesn't automatically make them lesbian.[34] When a person just doesn't feel like bothering with mates for a while, it doesn't automatically make them asexual. There is some part of all this which really does have to consider the big picture. Accordingly, each of the above definitions allows room for forays into other categories—which is why they're called preferences, not laws.

Group size

Sex, sexuality, and gender. Have we gotten them all? Nope. There are two more. You may have noticed that even though we've talked about initial preferences, we haven't said anything about bond maintenance or circumstances. While we're about to talk about heteronormativity, we can't do that without introducing two more broad concepts: that of group size and that of sexual practice.

Monogamy is the **preference for one mate at a time**

Polygamy is the **preference for multiple mates at a time**

Celibacy is the **preference for no mates** (though you can still have bonds).

Group size refers **the number of mates you prefer to have at once**. The Western heteronormative world privileges monogamy above all else. And I think that's a damned shame.

Group size may seem like a minor thing, until you consider that most of the commonly attended public-worthy deeds of a 21st century person in relationships have to do with the expectations for group size rather than sex, sexuality or gender. Cheating, dating, being unpartnered, promiscuity, marriage, and "family weigh-in" all assume certain things about exclusivity in relationships. But I've met far more girls who have cheated—and proudly told me so—than I can count. What does this mean for American females? It means that something about the story we tell regarding men and women in a commitment is either untrue, exaggerated, or at least suppressive of actual happenings. What does this mean for feminism? It means that, when feminists push for equal rights with a certain level of extra gusto, I and other men am filled with something you might not expect: distrust. Because "I know for certain" from personal experience that if I give a woman an inch in my system she'll take a mile. "I've seen *Sex in the City*," the man says. "You chicks are shameless. And now you want *more* rights?" Nowhere are rules more apt to be broken than in the realm of group size and what happens in those groups. Again, we know that men cheat too. But the brand of media scandal associated with this kind of thing is so much more in-your-face for high level men than it is for women, regardless of how long ago it happened. That is, the punishment is amplified for men. [35] Why is that? I suspect that it has something to do with the (perhaps unrealistic) heteronormative pressure for guarded exclusivity. And human male's ancient inclination towards the harem.[36],

Clearly men commit all kinds of crimes against women, but that's an issue less directly related to the discussion of group size. I've already discussed a little of this in previous chapters.

Before we leave the topic of group size, I'd also like to introduce a special category which may be useful for more of us to know about:

Strict Polygamy is the **preference for any number of mates at a time EXCEPT for one**

For various reasons in a person's psychology, monogamy (mono) may simply not work. Earlier I described myself as a "serial emotional cheater," and was so unable to remain physically and romantically exclusive with a partner that I would not—and still won't—commit exclusively to this day. The feeling is something like having a bowl of chips suddenly put in your face where previously there was nothing. And now you ask me to pick only *one* chip? Really? For some people, partners arrive in multiples, only work in multiples, and fail otherwise. This may especially apply to you if you notice certain patterns outside of relationships:

Two bosses, two bffs, four business partners, and nothing but fights with that one new sweetheart of yours—as always. If this sounds like you, not only might you be better suited for polygamy as a group number, you might be better suited for strict polygamy. Not because you want to be a player or a two-timer, but because—in the romantic context—you might do better *relating to a relationship* between people than you do *relating to the* `people` themselves. See the note in "Chapter 2: How a Male Becomes Feminist, On Non-standard Relationships" for how to understand this in yourself or your partner. As with being bisexual, strict polygamy is not nearly as easy to come to terms with as our giggly, yet shaming American public might think it is.

(Remember, in this context poly*gamy* refers to the number you *formally commit to*. Poly*amory* refers to the number you *bond with* whether or not you're formally committed.

- Intimate, non-formalized "-tuples" are polyamorous but not polygamist.
- Loveless harems are polygamist but not polyamorous.
- "Polycule" relationships recognized among three or more are both polygamously committed and polyamorous.)

Sexual practice

We have your biology (sex), your biologically-related identity (sexuality), your preference for other identities (gender), and the magic number which constrains the promises you make to those other identities (group number). The last topic we need to cover concerns how you prefer to play out your bonds with others.

Sexual practice describes **your preferences for expressing your bonds to your mates**.

I believe that the number one determinant of sexual compatibility between two mates is that of sexual practice. Just because you're a straight female and your dude's a straight male doesn't mean you'll work as a couple. Nor does two people being bisexual make them partners for life. Sexual practice encompasses all the fun stuff that makes the porn industry go. Swinging, stockings, blondes, rope bondage, tickling, sexting, whatever. There are too many categories to list here, but there's a very good reason for including this broad category in our toolset for feminism:

If I had to pick THE moment when I knew I had chosen something feminine as a key part of my identity, it would be when I adopted non-religious Daoism around age 26. I said to myself, *I'm choosing to follow a philosophy which doesn't preach, doesn't punish sins, doesn't reward with Heaven or threaten with Hell. It's so much...calmer than the Christianity I grew up with*. Here, I felt that I really was abandoning the whole "be a bold colonizer" kind of culture which a forward male was supposed to display. My intentional abandonment of macho pressures was further helped when I discovered poly and started meeting all of these people who respected others and talked about the importance of great communication all day. I was helped beyond the point of no return when some BDSM players in the poly group explained basic

BDSM to me, and finalized when, while writing my books on astrology, I found I had to think of sex not in terms of biology but in terms of patterns of interactions. All of this really derailed my previous notions of sex and power and convinced me, about a year before writing this current book, that my definition of my own masculinity had become a thing of my own making, that it intentionally ignored a lot of the bullshit I had previously been taught to swallow, and yet hadn't compromised my sense of male pride in any way. It *had* increased my willingness to contribute something to society via the things I loved most: free-scholarship, pattern-solving, and good relationships with others.

Essential to my interest in active feminism was a defiance of traditional notions of sexuality. As a hormone-enslaved male, I may not be as drawn to advocacy for rights from a female perspective I'll never know, but I do know that, as soon as I click that link to smoke and breath play and like what I'm seeing, I've joined a population of men who's basic preferences would get them shunned by their family and friends. We men like sex. We like being turned on. I hear that women do too. But when we prefer weird things, we also put ourselves on an island which we must forever hide from the "normal" world. Does this kind of thing actually help push a man towards feminism? It did for me. Because, in my arrogance I said things like, *This video is awesome. The fact that I can't really talk to my friends about it is bullshit. Niggaz iz squeamish, bruh.* At that point, you as the "deviant" male take on three new opponents which you broadly share with feminists: patriarchal society, heteronormative friends, and template-wielding partners. Gay or not, you have a choice to "out" yourself. Conflicted or not, you take your secret back to work with you the next day in a world which won't give you any acceptable outlet for expressing the identity you actually experience. In this sense, I was again fortunate to be a black male, because I already knew how the self-suppression thing worked. It seems like a raw deal, though, for a grown person not to be able to talk to his grown friends about certain grown things.

My point is not to convince you that feminists have a good market among perverts. I do aim to convince you that one way to make a man feel a kind of sexual oppression that he's disinclined to appreciate—one way to make him feel punished for something that he not only has a legal right to, but which forms a personal outlet for his normal biology—is to force him to submit to systems of sexual expression which aren't his. You can also do it by showing that you have no interest in what his personal preferences might be. The "pervert" label by the way isn't any more fair than calling someone a faggot, nigger, or a dike because of some vague story you heard about how "their kind" lives. Fourth wave feminism's central cause involves principles which can be extended to all realms of power, including that power to express one's identity in appropriate circumstances without suffering from others' ignorance. Although I don't plan to air any porn in front of the family or colleagues any time soon, I do plan to keep pursuing a society which is more capable of tackling taboo issues without falling back on uncritical giggles and scarlet letters.

Obstructions to the feminist agenda

Heteronormativity

The social practice for measuring people's behaviors against heterosexual standards is called **heteronormativity**. Some of the key assumptions of heteronormativity are as follows:

- Males should be masculine, females should be feminine, and most people should, when they come to maturity, be heterosexual.

- When in doubt, masculinity supersedes femininity.

- Monogamy is the preferred group number. Other numbers are generally considered deviant. Even celibacy.

- Sex between a monogamous, heterosexual couple is a private matter, but a society has the right to give its opinion on any non-vanilla (non-plain) sexual practice which becomes known to others.

- We don't typically talk about non-vanilla practice, but will suggest such practices in media if it drives sales.

- Non-hetero, non-monogamous arrangements are assumed to be dysfunctional compared to their hetero and mono alternatives unless or until sufficient science or years of public desensitizing media depictions suggest otherwise.[37]

- Normal, hetero-approved groups can deny, curb, or suspend the expressive or legal rights of non-heteronormative groups—usually via moral arguments like "we think it damages the child," "the normal public shouldn't pay for it," or "it's indecent."

Now, from an evolutionary and a sociological perspective, heteronormativity is basically good, because it provides a much-needed system of behavioral rules through which the masses without badges can keep weird elements in check. Heteronormativity also represents a set of cultural-evolutionary "best practices." In the same way that we now describe kin-mating as gross (because people who did it had a higher chance of bearing children with family-specific mutations), we also say that heterosexuality is cool (because people who do it, in theory, produce children for the propagation of the human species). As humans have seen bad stuff happen because of science they couldn't yet explain, they've told social stories suggesting other humans not go there. Or try to behave so they won't have to go there. In this sense, heteronormativity stabilizes a culture's practice for that culture's very broad stability.

The problem with heteronormativity is that one size really doesn't fit all. Some people rage out under monogamy. Some people just aren't heterosexual. Some people's upbringing truly has altered what would have been "acceptable" approaches to things, and in cases like this, we would like to have a society which provided outlets for this. My main disappointment in heteronormativity isn't so much that it exists, but that we know *so much* about the exceptions that you would think a sufficiently educated society would do something other than retweet its template-trained censorship of alternative practices which everyone knows are there. Maybe I'm just naïve in these matters. In any event, where you have heteronormativity, you typically have **Othering: treating alternatives to a standard as if they are "not that standard" rather than allowing the alternatives to have identities of their own**. Women, ethnic power subjects, the disabled, the elderly, and the poor are all treated as the Other under the heteronormative standard, because heterosexuality supersedes alternative genders, masculinity supersedes femininity under heterosexuality, and masculine power holders tend to prioritize the topics that interest them. Either because they are not comparatively masculine, not socially powerful, or both, the Othered groups are more likely to gain cultural attention only when they do things which immediately affect the masculine power holders' interests. Most of the time this isn't happening though, so heteronormative society is less likely to advocate for these groups' rights.

I still find it strange that the heterosexual standard can be linked to social oppression.[38] But it's not so strange once we frame the heterosexual standard as a broader set of rules for exercising power among actors.

Patriarchy

Patriarchy has less to do with men specifically and more to do with the perpetuation of masculine-elements in a system. It isn't just a matter of men hiring and promoting each other (a practice which has been changing for a couple of decades now), but a matter of masculine institutional standards reinforcing themselves. For example, when a school district stops distributing textbooks because it claims to have plans for replacing these books with technology—when it does this without having consulted the teachers who must now teach everything themselves without a formal aid, without having consulted the parents whose children must accept their education from that single teacher, without having actually installed the infrastructure for supporting or even switching to the technology they claimed in a timely manner—this is patriarchy. My middle brother Keith actually encountered this while subbing at a local high school:

> Keith: So let me get this straight. They stopped giving you guys books?
>
> Student: Yeah. We haven't had books in a while. Since before last year.
>
> Keith: So how do you do homework?
>
> Student: Miss just assigns us stuff or gets it off the web.
>
> Keith: Well how do you take notes?

Student: Miss just gives us hers or tells us to write
it down.

Keith: Oookay. But didn't you say you leave
those notes here at school?

Student: Yeah.

Keith: But how do you study?

Student: If Miss doesn't teach us, (*shrug*) we
just don't know it.

Although I typically try not to get too opinionated over
political matters, I've told several people that—of all the
political decisions I've heard on *any* level for as long as
I've been alive—stopping the distribution of textbooks in
schools without having already introduced sufficient
backup material is the worst decision I've ever heard.
Later I asked one of my college students about this and he
said that his school district actually did hand out laptops
instead, but 1) this has been the exception in my city as far
as I've heard and 2) even if the switch to technology were
successfully completed in every school, a move like this
put the onus on every teacher to scour the web for a full
year's worth of curriculum and instructional materials.
Once located, you still have to integrate these resources
into your curriculum. You still have to learn where to find

the solutions without letting your students find them first. You still need a system for grading, tracking, and threading the lessons together. As a teacher myself, I find the whole idea disgusting. And then people have the nerve to call for "master teachers." Hmph. *You* try being the sole source of knowledge for hundreds of students, 180 days a year, without reliable support material. *You* try taking the blame from parents and administrators on either side when their kids aren't learning.

Broadly framed, textbook suspension is an issue of people deciding to follow the cultural inertia without regard for those on the frontline who must pay for that decision. I'm not a parent, but knowing of my own challenges in the classroom with personalities alone, I wouldn't trust a single teacher without a reliable cross-reference to teach all of US History to my child. This kind of follow-the-blind practice punishes both the teacher and the students. All for what? So that districts can save money while passing it off as "technologizing." Such is the irresponsible acting-receiving decision-making of patriarchy: "We'll just cut out books. It's the teachers' job to teach. They'll just use the web until we get some kind of laptop thing in place. It's their job to give notes to the students." Irresponsible.

Patriarchy is **a social structure which privileges the power**

holder's right to constrain the identities and processes of those subject to that power. This is the institutional extension two things: masculine dominance display amidst uncertainty and masculine "action first, feedback second." Because this is a social structure, the idea that patriarchy perpetuates itself is already built in.

Perhaps you can imagine that you don't actually need a room full of men in order to have a patriarchy. US education agencies on the state level have plenty of women in them and yet are bureacratically patriarchal by design (with legislation like No Child Left Behind and ESSA,[39] their associated accountability cultures, and by virtue of their role as an umbrella for their states' schools in general). Patriarchy can also be found on the family level in systems where the dad and the sons rule the family dynamics. This second example is more neutral in its effects, though.

Like most social phenomena, patriarchy doesn't have to be a bad thing. Especially in cases where the power subjects are underequipped to define their own roles properly, patriarchies like the Medieval Catholic Church and the Egyptian pharaonic system serve to organize people and enrich the collective where the people themselves would be too scattered to do so. One might even argue that, assuming Americans' media addiction and inability to influence their local governments (like school boards) on even the most basic level, we Americans *deserve* a patriarchy. But this is a reflection of our citizens' impotence more than it is a reflection of the power holders themselves.

How do we know it's us and not "the patriarchs" who are to blame when a system goes wrong? Because no matter who's President of the country, missile politics and speech-making continue to command a higher priority than forward social policy. No matter who's on our school boards, you'll still hear parents lamenting the state of public education. No matter how expensive we complain things get, we still happily buy those things when the urge hits us. If patriarchy (in the dysfunctional sense) is self-perpetuating, it is because we don't have enough people passing through such systems who are able to stop and rewrite those systems. If you've ever been promoted in a system which you knew was broken before your promotion, you know how this works. It's really easy to simply merge into that broken system isn't it? As long as the paycheck continues to come, right? Such is patriarchy.

If feminism can be said to have an enemy, I argue that the enemy should be a combination of heteronormativity and unchallenged patriarchy. Some might say that sexism is the enemy, and perhaps this was so in the 1960s. Today, however, you're less likely to run into an openly sexist male and more likely to simply run into an ignorant male. Worse still, you are less likely to run into a sexist female and more likely to run into a sexist-trained female—such that the masculine-template, culture of dismissiveness, and uncritical assumptions about how males and females should behave are reinforced by males and females alike. This is worse not because women also reinforce the standards of sexism as men do, but because *both* men and women are reinforcing the *patriarchal* standards that underlie sexism.

What heteronormativity and unchecked patriarchy have in common is the idea that it's okay to show both men and women, blues and blacks, rich and poor, corporation and consumer side by side, but it's not okay to challenge the processes by which those pairs' interests continue to clash. Those processes continue to favor the masculine style of dominance in the dark. What we don't know, we don't bother to know. But we will imprison it. Behaviorally, conceptually, literally, or some combination of these. And while it remains true that societies require structure—ours may even require both heteronormativity and patriarchy—such structure damages itself when it resorts to its own tactics to prevent itself from being changed.

Like a boxer who'd rather saw off his own arm than get punched there, unchecked heteronormativity encourages a disconnected social space as increasing percentages of the population discover that they prefer things they were told they shouldn't prefer—breaking off into subgroups that defy the structure of their original support networks. Unchecked patriarchy encourages a rigidly inadaptable rule structure as these marginalized groups continue to disperse in their interests, yet are presumed to still be governable by systems that cannot unite them. Thanks largely to great advances in the technology of person-to-person communication and business-to-consumer customization, we no longer have to settle on false collective-identity narratives. Not everyone is a straight Christian. Not everyone trusts the government. Not everyone dreams of the white picket fence. And now that we have greater access to people who feel as we do, we don't all have to pretend to prefer these things anymore. No one does. Can heteronormativity retain its right to constrain people's private preferences when so many of the people who used to swear by it have long abandoned many of its basic prescriptions? Is unchecked patriarchy really justified when, despite all of the economic prosperity it has brought us, social quality of life and overall happiness in the US continues, by many measures, to drop on average as the years go on?[40,41,42,a]

Summary

In this chapter I outlined one conception of feminism and some ideas related to it. Although the topic of feminism extends far beyond sex, feminism's roots in the struggle for male-female equality led us to consider several dimensions of maleness and femaleness. Here, I had to distinguish between male and female biologies, processes, and "preferences." I also argued that many of the rules for how we form relationships are subject to the all-judging rule of monogamy. Monogamy was one of the major assumptions of heteronormativity which, alongside patriarchy, constituted a system for boxing in much of the feminist agenda. Old school sexism still exists, but has largely gone out of style and been replaced with more subtle, yet more insidious assumptions about how social actors should subject themselves to others' power. Such assumptions have a way of getting into the minds of these

---

[a] The overall data on the quality of life in the U.S. are a mixed bag, depending on what we measure and who measures it. Although the sources show that the situation in the States isn't nearly as bad as some argue (all things considered), the country's social measures and enduring inequity continue to cap its overall rankings.

social actors and encouraging them to persist on paths of expression that they themselves don't even recognize as valid.

Even if the basic goal of feminism is equality of the sexes, the sexes, as biologies, are simply not equal. Though we all know that this is not the kind of simplistic equality that is meant by feminism, it *is* the kind of equality that comes to mind when males and females discuss the subject. Connotation is the problem. In order to remove the biological connotations, I proposed a definition of feminism which revolves around the balancing of masculine- and feminine-type *processes*. This definition was less accurate as a description of what feminism actually is, but a more practical description for universalizing feminism's aims to include everyone's power interests. Even if feminism is, at its core, mostly about women, women themselves can only be described in a few ways: using biology, behavior, or social setup. By deemphasizing biology and emphasizing behavior and social setup in the definition, I aimed to explain why people besides women—especially the sexually and civically marginalized—should share in the feminist cause.

8. On Patriarchal Systems

The classic patriarchal system can be identified by its masculine-heavy characteristics. In line with my earlier description of masculine-elements, patriarchal systems favor intrusive features over accommodating ones, assertion over feedback, contrasts and differences over similarities, and centralized properties for defining how we viewers respond to those systems. Although most centralized governments and administrative systems are at least partly patriarchal as a consequence of their intrusive (but important) social-structuring functions, we don't normally consider those masculine elements to be damaging unless their functions serve to noticeably compromise the interests of the people they serve.

In line with the above, we can easily recognize systems that are negatively patriarchal. A family line whose power automatically passes from father to son might constitute a patriarchal lineage, but not negatively so unless (or until) the women in it begin to see themselves as being harmed by this. Organizations like the NFL or the Freemasons may be fundamentally male, but to the extent that they serve the whole community as well as each other—to the extent that they champion service, charity, and the social good—the biological masculine membership is strongly balanced by feminine-element, inclusive dynamics; so these would be far less likely to be considered patriarchies.

The US government, on the other hand, can be considered a struggling patriarchy. Our system has faced different versions of the same set of equality and equity issues, the same largely inaccessible system of power lobbies, the same perpetuation of class division in terms of legislative voice, and the same charisma-based personality marketing (above the issues) for as long as many of us can remember. To the extent that most of us Americans have become accustomed to taking what is given on most issues except for the few we agree on—more importantly, to the extent that we are generally okay with 1) not voting, 2) not feeling like our vote counts, or 3) voting mostly for names we know absolutely nothing about—our republic receives less of our informed individual feedback and force-feeds us more in the way of non-individual default (and nameless) "other" candidates; 30 positions to vote for and we've only really heard about five. We only care about two. We may or may not vote. But AARP knows who's running. It has a lobby. That lobby effectively votes. The people already in office know whose running. They likely have a decent idea of how they should vote. Unless we as citizens magically become organized

enough to vote for candidates who actually reflect our
local interests, we'll keep getting mostly candidates
handed to us by the existing lobby. Or straight party
extremes who embody our overall discontentment with
the previous guy.[43] We don't have a system of
representation so much as we have a system of reaction.
The rest is imposed by a very complex web spun of our
collective "not knowing and not bothering to know."
That's negative patriarchy: a rule of law asserted into our
civic lives without effective mechanisms for integrating
our own self-defined interests. Like so many
stuck-systems, it's less about The Man keeping you down
and more about the *collective* lacking proper institutional
structures for bringing you up. So no, it's not Trump or
Obama's fault. It's not the Democrats or Republicans
fault. It's just the system we've all grown up in, which
hasn't had enough of a critical mass of bold characters to
change.

If negative patriarchy forces identities from on high,
negative matriarchy blends identities into an inertia which
discourages non-conformity. Very few societal systems
in the world are truly matriarchal, but on the family level,
matriarchy appears to be the default. My own family line
is basically matriarchal, where the women of the line
largely determine the public and private identity of
everyone in the family (including the men). In my family

line, the women's professions outshine or pay more than those of the men, and the women set the family agenda through a more collectivist, council structure which measures progress against an already established set of norms. It does this more than would, say, a single leader-assertion system. Like patriarchy though, matriarchy only becomes negative if it harms the people in it. The system works in my family line, but not so much in the determination of school curriculum, for example.

If you've ever taught K-12, you know that school districts tend to be patriarchal in their bureaucracy, but matriarchal in their pedagogy; On the one hand, "The Man"—fearing that he might lose funding—has robbed his teachers of much of their classroom control. On the other hand, the Education Board—wishing to keep up with the latest thing—has imposed another academic fad upon all teachers in the system. The latest acronym. The latest multiple-learning method. The newest "smarterizing," equalizing, accountability initiative. As a teacher, you were likely never asked whether Common Core made sense; some council somewhere simply absorbed it into your classroom on your behalf. Nobody asked you if RATEY was better or worse for teaching conic sections. A well-meaning collective discussion simply produced it as the new standard. Maybe these systems are good for your class. Maybe they're not, but by means of a read-only, feminine-element process, you are once again responsible for filling in all the gaps for implementing yet another new thing—not just for your students, but for yourself and for your school (which likely didn't give you everything you needed to regroup effectively.)

Because our public systems are like this, we now have a system of academies whose main selling point isn't so much that they're good, but that they're 1) not public and 2) attentive to many of the old systems of school cultural control which our public systems have forgotten about. Thanks to their negatively patriarchal bureaucratic sides, our public school systems are increasingly occupied with newer facilities and accountability numbers more than they are on actual student fates. At least the academies advertise a "concern" for whether their students turn out to be good people. Not just asses in chairs who'll refrain from suing.

Related to the issues of K-12, we have a general postsecondary system focused on three major messages:

- Everyone should get a degree because you're nobody if you don't have one.

- Schools need innovative ways to make money because the student loan system is rich which

hypothetical value made actual, but not if you
lose your market to some online thing.

- We're paying more attention to student-focused
  outcomes such as jobs and soft-skills because the
  K-12 system has handed them to us unprepared
  for real life consequences.

Of the three messages above, the third one is pretty noble,
the second one is more of a practical reality, and the first
one is the byproduct of the template-planting society we
live in.

Actually, the idea that all Americans should have a
college degree—whether or not they've emerged with
truly college-level learning—wouldn't be so bad if not for
its implications for the broader worth of the individual.
Combined with persistent media images, sharpened social
marketing, and an overall climate of grand peer pressure,
an early 21st century US citizen gets the general idea that
he or she, must be rich, smiling, sassily or flippantly
confident, and ever on vacation. By tying success to a
select array of tangible, marketable objects, we've also
instilled in ourselves the notion that a person without the
beach as his context, a degree as his knowledge, or
irreverence as his action, has not "made it" in the world.
That too is negative patriarchy; Father Media has told us

everything we need to be. How dare we find contentment with our lives some other way.

The implications for feminism

Recall that fourth wave feminism is mainly about self-acceptance. If there's one thing we can get out of our pervasively patriarchal systems (alongside matriarchy in the case of education), it's that institutions which are extreme in how we interact with them are often institutions which are incapable of adapting to those of us whom they serve. Now that tech connects us so heavily, you would think that we could share knowledge for creating better institutions, not just bigger ones. Because, however, we remain locked in old animal-style fears and insecurities—because we still need social approval and stable life circumstances for our lowest Maslowian needs, it's pretty easy to convince us that the world beyond the box is damned dangerous. You can't vote for the Libertarians even though they make sense. You can't be okay without a degree even though you're perfectly fine with your own hustle. You can't have that non-paying hobby even though everyone around you, who *completely* gave theirs up for pay, now hates what they do. You can't be okay with Trump AND Obama. If you're not enraged at one of them then the person you're talking to is enraged at your lack of rage. And no you for damn sure can't try to understand the white supremacist, the feminist, the pro-lifer, the Democrat, or anyone else not on the side of our favorite clique. We, men AND women, patriarchally assert that divisiveness is the only way. Even if divisiveness doesn't suit you. Even if you're tired of all the angry people around you. Whether or not you just want to enjoy the civil company of civil people around you without having to dodge the larger world. What does feminism have to do with it? If the missiles are all we know, if the "strong crushing the weak" is our only paradigm, then self-acceptance ceases to be viable as we ourselves realize we're under the thumb of collectives we couldn't possible outyell. Beyond individual interests, the cause of equality has implications not only for our own society today, but for the process that will build our loved one's society tomorrow.

For those interested in advancing the fourth wave on a more collective level, we have an immediate route for men and one for women. Female feminists will likely benefit from more actively welcoming dialogue with men interested in equality; despite how easy it may be to think of feminist action in terms of women-populated assembly, there are males inside and outside of the political sphere who abhor domestic violence, who are embarrassed by the low numbers of women in legislation, who would love to fix a number of society's domestic issues if only there were more sane voices to work with. But feminists as a girls' only club doesn't help any of this.

It's not really expected that many men will claim feminism any time soon, but the title doesn't matter. The *objective* is what's most important. True equality doesn't take a lot of work to imagine: Men who can interact with women respectfully and openly, listening without feeling that they're weak for doing so, and remaining mindful of when we have certain advantages that women don't have…That's part of the man's equation. The other part, for those of us feeling assaulted in the current times, may be even more important: Expect the same kind of respect from your partners and employers that you would from your son and your male friends. If you wouldn't stand being cut down by the latter, don't let yourself take it from the former. You don't have to tell them off, but you don't have to bow to that kind of thing either. By asserting our right to be respected as people, we avoid the frustration of feeling trapped by all those male-defining factors beyond our control—the ones that take away our options. To support the fourth wave broadly, men should establish the basis for equal respect in personal relationships while women establish such a basis in tolerant social alliances. This might seem backwards until you look at what we currently accept as Westerners: There are more than enough opportunities for women to injure men socially and more than enough opportunities for men to limit women behaviorally. As with all two-sided power, the goal is also for those who have it to wield it justly—not just for those who want it to strive for more.

9. Conclusion

I began writing this book in a very different place from where I ended up a year later. Initially a respect-seeking second waver reacting to what he saw as an abuse of girl-power levied upon him, I evolved into a fourth waver who knows that a whole lot of problems go away if you simply respect yourself and your unique strengths. As surely as $1+1=2$, your fully expressed character isn't something that anyone can call into question. I think that the ultimate source of modern American angst is that we all have too many opinions demanding that we place others' ideal selves over our own. We have too few opportunities to truly tune out the noise of countless unhappy people riding the rage train. We have too many occasions for listening to the suggestions of people who know nothing about us—people who are less interested in whether *we* thrive and more interest in broadcasting *their* various concerns to anyone who'll hear them. To maintain our place in those unhappy worlds, we believe that we must participate in everyone else's bitter striving in order to keep their approval. But something happens once you start respecting the person you see in the mirror.

Finding a respect for strengths you really do have, you say things like

- I know my class has its pros and cons in others' eyes, but I don't have to apologize for being [White/Black/Hispanic/…].

- I'm proud to be male, but because I know what that means, I don't need to oppress others in the way that I wouldn't want to be oppressed.

- I don't need to listen to the advice of someone who can't take their own. I don't need to accept anger from people who are never happy. I don't need to give up value to a system that never has enough.

- I've earned better company.

- I'm happy enough with myself to focus on helping to others instead.

Locked in the old view of activism, many people still believe that you're not really out for change unless you're protesting against something somewhere. Unless you're setting a car on fire. Unless you vocally and disgruntledly remind everyone of how oppressed your class is, and how pissed you are as a result. But that's the old way of seeing

things. Modern civic rules tell us that protest isn't policy.
Man hate isn't equality. White-shaming won't bring
black justice. You live in the same society I do; although
there is something to be said for calling out injustices
where we see them, there's no long term merit in
assuming that 99% of the other people out there are
equally unjust. Class division is both a protection against
outside threat and a prison amidst outside benefits.[44] The
new activism of two-sided issue resolution is as important
(and inevitable) for our behavioral structures as the legal
system has been for our community structures. And not
all activism needs to be public: As men and women alike
can attest, a public actor who isn't right with himself in
private may do everyone a big favor by staying home. I
don't need a messed up person jeopardizing my whole
team's cause.

One of the strongest bases of open division among people
is that of visible differences. Countries have different
flags; teams where different uniforms; ethnicities have
different appearances. Ours is the challenge of gathering
those differences to produce a league worth
following—whether it's a soccer league, a league of
nations, or a league of extraordinary gentlemen. Visible
differences, used beneficially, give us access to entire
packages of impression which we simply couldn't access
on our own. As a native San Antonian, I've had a genuine

love-hate track record with the Latinas in my life, but all in all the cultural stereotype of fire and family is one I wouldn't trade. Whites present me with a constant reminder of how many assumptions are stacked against me in a new place before I've gotten my footing; go figure that as person who loves taking on difficult, underestimated, and thought-heavy subjects, most of my friends are white, some are poor, many are rich; and almost all are women. My black friends still charge up crowds, but they do it as artists—working to be pioneers in their field. And each person represents a piece of the outlook I've built towards life. Whether you take the good or the bad from the classes in your life is your choice.

Your visual look raises awareness of others' attitudes about your class. The visual look of your friends reflects the attitude you prefer in others, along with how you prefer to interact with such an attitude. You can hate another class and exclude them all day, but the attitude which that class represents to you is YOUR OWN. So you can think of us Blacks as noisy in groups or get excited by the noise we instill in groups, but even when we're absent, how you handle charged groups in your own life will reflect whatever attitude you've chosen to dish out; you'll pay or be rewarded accordingly. You can think of men as useless pigs or women as sources of endless tumult, but even when they are absent, how you

handle sudden destabilizing events (masculine-element)
or systems which require a whole collection of roles
beyond your special part (feminine-element) will dog
your life until you get your stuff together.

To be a White abolitionist, a Black peacemaker, a male
feminist, a peaceful warrior, is to see the value in those
things against which we define ourselves. To truly get
past the issues that ail us, we may need to act as we never
have. To do that, we'll need to draw from sources we've
formerly excluded, so that the full array of tools becomes
available to us.

I hope you've gotten as much out of reading this as I have
in the year spent writing it, and hope your future battles
will quell needless anger beneath the enjoyment of your
full skill.

References

Chapter 1. My First Encounters with Feminism

[1] Smith, A., & Cannan, E. (1776/2003). *The wealth of nations*. New York, N.Y: Bantam Classic.

[2] De Wolf, P. (2015). Male feminism: Men's participation in women's emancipation movements and debates. Case studies from Belgium and France (1967–1984). *European Review of History*, *22*(1), 77–100.

Chapter 2. How a Male Becomes Feminist

[3] Johnson, O. S. (2005). *The sexual spectrum: Exploring human diversity*. Raincoast Books.

[4] Abbot, E. (2000). *A history of celibacy*. Simon and Schuster, 2000

[5] Butler, J. (2009). Performativity, precarity and sexual politics. *AIBR. Revista de Antropología Iberoamericana*, *4*(3), 309.

Chapter 4. Black Male Feminist

[6] Center for American Women in Politics (2018). *Women in Congress 2018*. Retrieved from http://www.cawp.rutgers.edu/women-us-congress-2018.

[7] Institute for Women's Policy Research (2018). *Pay equity & discrimination*. Retrieved from https://iwpr.org/issue/employment-education-economic-change/pay-equity-discrimination/

[8] Fredrickson, B. L., & Roberts, T. (1997). Objectification theory: Towards understanding women's lived experiences

and mental health risks. *Psychology of Women Quarterly, 21*, 173–206.

[9] Douglas, S. J., & Michaels, M. W. (2004). *The mommy myth: The idealization of motherhood and how it has undermined women*. New York: Free Press.

[10] de Beauvoir, S. (1949/1989). *The second sex*. (Dell Williams papers.) New York: Vintage Books.

Chapter 5. A Short Note on Feminism's Four Waves

[11] National Women's History Museum (n.d.). *Elizabeth Cady Stanton*. Retrieved from https://www.womenshistory.org/education-resources/biographies/elizabeth-cady-stanton

[12] Lunardini, C., & Knock, T. (1980). Woodrow Wilson and woman suffrage: A new look. *Political Science Quarterly, 95*(4), 655-671. doi:10.2307/2150609

[13] Irigaray, L. (1974/1985). *Speculum of the other woman*, trans. G. C. Gill, Ithaca: Cornell University Press.

[14] Zakin, E. (2011). *Psychoanalytic feminism*. Retrieved from https://plato.stanford.edu/entries/feminism-psychoanalysis/

[15] Gerhard, J. F. (2001). *Desiring revolution: Second-wave feminism and the rewriting of American sexual thought, 1920 to 1982*. New York: Columbia University Press.

[16] National Conference of State Legistlatures. (2014). *Affirmative action: Overview*. Retrieved from http://www.ncsl.org/research/education/affirmative-action-overview.aspx

[17] Mann, S., & Huffman, D. (2005). The decentering of second wave feminism and the rise of the third wave. *Science & Society, 69*(1), 56-91.

[18] Rampton, M. (2008/2015). *Four waves of feminism*. Retrieved from https://www.pacificu.edu/about/media/four-waves-feminism

[19] Solee, K. (2015). 6 things to know about 4th wave feminism. Retrieved from https://www.bustle.com/articles/119524-6-things-to-know-about-4th-wave-feminism

Chapter 6. On Abuse and Domestic Violence

[20] World Health Organization (2007). *Engaging men and boys in changing gender-based inequity in health: Evidence from programme interventions*. Geneva. Retrieved from https://www.who.int/gender/documents/Engaging_men_bo ys.pdf

[21] Scottish Government (2008). *Theories used to explain male violence against women partners and ex-partners*. Retrieved from https://www2.gov.scot/resource/doc/925/0063072.pdf

[22] Santos, R. A., & Alfred, M. V. (2016). Literacy, parental roles, and support systems among single latino father families. *Journal of Research & Practice for Adult Literacy, Secondary & Basic Education, 5*(3), 5–17.

[23] Hess, M., Ittel, A., & Sisler, A. (2014). Gender-specific macro- and micro-level processes in the transmission of gender role orientation in adolescence: The role of fathers. *European Journal of Developmental Psychology, 11*(2), 211–226.

Chapter 7. One Man's Understanding of Sex, Gender, and Feminism

[24] Oxford Living Dictionaries (2018). *Feminism*. Retrieved from https://en.oxforddictionaries.com/definition/feminism

[25] Jones, A.G., & Ratterman, N.L. (2009). Mate choice and sexual selection: what have we learned since Darwin? *Proceedings of the National Academy of Sciences of the United States of America, 106* Suppl 1, 10001-8.

[26] Fink, B., & Neave, N. (2005). The biology of facial beauty. *International Journal of Cosmetic Science, 27*(6), 317–325.

[27] Ruggiero, V. R. (1999). *Becoming a critical thinker*. Boston: Houghton Mifflin.

[28] Butler, J. (1990). *Gender trouble: Feminism and the subversion of identity*, New York: Routledge.

[29] Koyama, E. (2003). The transfeminist manifesto. In R. Dicker & A. Piepmeier (Ed.), *Catching a wave: Reclaiming feminism for the twenty-first century*. Northeastern University Press

[30] Stein, P. L., & Rowe, B. M. (2014). *Physical anthropology*.

[31] Viero, C., Shibuya, I., Kitamura, N., Verkhratsky, A., Fujihara, H., Katoh, A., … Dayanithi, G. (2010). Oxytocin: crossing the bridge between basic science and pharmacotherapy. *CNS Neuroscience & Therapeutics, 16*(5), e138–e156.

[32] Kadushin, C. (2012). *Understanding social networks: Concepts, theories, and findings*. New York: Oxford University Press.

[33] GLAAD (n.d.) *GLAAD media reference guide – transgender*. Retrieved from https://www.glaad.org/reference/transgender.

[34] Johnson, O. S. (2005). *The sexual spectrum: Exploring human diversity*. Raincoast Books.

[35] Wypijewski, J. (2018). What we don't talk about when we talk about... *Nation, 306*(8), 12–18.

[36] Lewis, H. (2018). The year women said: Me Too. *New Statesman, 147*(5440), 30–32.

[37] Yue, A. (2014). Queer Asian cinema and media studies: From hybridity to critical regionality. *Cinema Journal, 53*(2), 145–151.

[38] Hubbard, P. (2000). Desire/disgust: mapping the moral contours of heterosexuality. *Progress in Human Geography, 24*(2), 191–217.

[39] US Department of Education (n.d.) *Every Student Succeeds Act (ESSA)*. Retrieved from https://www.ed.gov/essa

[40] Washington Post. (2018). *Perhaps tired of winning, the United States falls in World Happiness rankings—again.* Retrieved from https://www.washingtonpost.com/ news/worldviews/wp/2018/03/14/perhaps-tired-of-winning -the-united-states-falls-in-world-happiness-rankings-again/

[41] United Nations Development Programme (2018). *Human development indices and indicators: 2018 statistical update* Retrieved from http://hdr.undp.org/sites/default/files/ 2018_human_development_statistical_update.pdf

[42] Legatum Institute (2008/2018). *Legatum Prosperity Index*. Retrieved from https://www.prosperity.com/

Chapter 8. On Patriarchal Systems

[43] Key Jr, V. O. (1955). A theory of critical elections. *The Journal of Politics, 17*(1), 3-18.

Chapter 9. Conclusion

[44] Granovetter, M. (2005). The impact of social structure on economic outcomes. *Journal of economic perspectives*, *19*(1), 33-50.

www.ingramcontent.com/pod-product-compliance
Lightning Source LLC
Chambersburg PA
CBHW060336030426
42336CB00011B/1367